# From Barbados
# to
# Banffshire

## (Via Guyana)

A Family Story Spanning Six Generations
Across the Atlantic Ocean

## Christine A.F. Wilkie

# From Barbados to Banffshire

Published by: Pennyfeu Productions

Front cover design by Rhona Wilkie
Front cover photographs:
Upper: Part of mural by Neville "Oluyemi" Legall on wall (now demolished)
at Rock Hall free village memorial site, Barbados
Lower: Author's father on top of corn ricks at his farm at Rothiemay, Banffshire

Colour insert photographs:
Stain glass window, St. Georges Cathedral, St Vincent and the Grenadines
Kaieteur Falls, Potaro River, Kaieteur National Park, Guyana

ISBN: 978-1-7393279-0-3

**From Barbados to Banffshire**

*In Loving Memory of my parents
Constance Margot Turpin Weir
& Alexander Thomas Weir*

This book has been compiled for the benefit of the next generation especially:

Owen, Roisin, Christina, Elsa, Alexander, Wilbur and Penelope

as well as descendants of the families of Turpin, Grant, Gray, Rowley, Weir, Turner, Webster and McEwan.

# From Barbados to Banffshire

# Contents                                                    Page

# Introduction

My decision to write this book has been inspired by my desire to find out about my family's unspoken mixed ethnicity. This was specifically in relation to my mother's paternal ancestors who were concentrated in the West Indies, particularly Barbados.

I am the second oldest in a family of five girls. We are, in chronological order of birth, Margaret, me, Gladys, Betty and Avril. Margaret, Gladys and I were all born in Guyana. Betty and Avril were born in Scotland.

All my mother's generation had passed away by the time I made any serious effort to find out more than what I already knew. I joined Ancestry.com in November 2017 and had a DNA test which in the first analysis I received, revealed mainly Scottish/English ethnicity, but the 2% West African was what made the research a must do for me (see Appendix 4 for a more recent analysis).

I had built in my mind quite an idyllic view of the land of my maternal ancestors through visiting the tropical Islands of Barbados, Trinidad, Tobago, St Vincent and the Grenadines as well as Guyana. My husband David Wilkie (Dave) and I would enjoy swimming in the warm seas and revelling in the relaxing ambiance of these places. However, while we were aware that slavery, that dark and dreadful humanitarian disgrace, still haunted these islands as well as Guyana, we had not imagined that my ancestors had any involvement in anything so horrible.

My intent is that this book will give our descendants a more accurate picture of who we are. It should help to explain why our family is so "far-flung" and scattered throughout the globe, from Australia and New Zealand to the USA, the West Indies and the British Isles. My friends and their friends have often said that the history of my family would be fascinating to read. I had no idea how correct they were.

1

# From Barbados to Banffshire

**"Truth is always better than fiction.... you have, slavery, sex with slave women, freedom, murder, intrigue, empowerment, Christ and the church"** ....... That is the book I want to read.

These are the words of Sandra Taitt-Eaddy, who is an expert on Caribbean Genealogy. Sandra was born and brought up in Barbados and now lives in the USA. She expressed an interest in my story when I joined the Facebook group "Barbados Genealogy". Her knowledge of where to get information and her access to relevant records has been invaluable. This was the sort of encouragement I needed.

Towards the end of 2019 Dave and I arranged to visit Barbados to see what we could find out about my mother's great grandfather Joseph Turpin. My understanding of family lore led me to believe he had been a bishop.

Sandra gave me contact details for a colleague of hers, a retired Professor, Sir Woodville Marshall, who had an interest in the first free villages of Barbados, where the Turpin name had come up. The Professor has authored books and articles on the subject from which I have his permission to quote.

Through my genealogy research and with the help of Sandra and Sir Woodville, I now know that Joseph Turpin, my mother's great grandfather, was born into slavery. "The secret in the family!" Who knew the secret? This has to be one of the major factors which prompted me to become an author. I have been inspired by the very topical "Black Lives Matter" movement to own my African ancestry, limited as it is. I need to face up to the fact that slavery in the West Indies and beyond was brutal and should be addressed with some regret by people like me, who are of predominantly British descent.

# Introduction

The main inspiration for "From Barbados to Banffshire" has been my beloved mother, Constance Margot Turpin/Weir. She was born in Barbados in 1918 but lived most of her childhood between the country which was known at that time as British Guiana, where her parents lived, and Trinidad, where she went to school. Her father Milton, her grandfather Edmund and great grandfather Joseph were all born in Barbados. This story also includes information about family travels to the West Indian islands of St Vincent and the Grenadines, Trinidad & Tobago, Jamaica and the country of my birth, Guyana.

Although I have concentrated mostly on the Turpin side of my mother's family, I have also included what I know of the Grant/Van Buren history (my mother's paternal grandmother's family) and the Gray/Rowley history (her mother's family). I have also found out previously unknown family history gained through my membership of Ancestry.co.uk. I have had a few surprises there - not all good and some extremely sad, particularly with reference to the Gray family. The Grants, who were a slave owning family in St Vincent, are related to the Listers of Shibden Hall in Halifax. Anne Lister who wrote the secret diaries which inspired the BBC drama series "Gentleman Jack" shown in the UK is not my relative, but the family who inherited the property from her were related to my great grandmother Julia Grant/Turpin.

In this book I have also included my father, Alexander Thomas Weir's paternal family and in addition his maternal Webster family history. My father is responsible for the "Banffshire" in the book's title, having emigrated from there to British Guiana to "seek his fortune" in 1927. 20 years later he returned to Banffshire, (in Scotland), not with the kind of fortune he was seeking but with a chronic illness, a young wife and three very young children including myself. Through writing my father's story, I have learned quite a lot about him and his family. This was achieved mainly through going over my memories with those of my sisters and cousins. My father was an interesting if complex character. Writing about him has been a worthwhile experience which has helped me to come to terms

# From Barbados to Banffshire

with my rather complicated relationship with him. His life history has been a complete contrast to my mother's early life.

From the mid-19th century, the Anglican Church figures strongly in my family history with at least four clergymen in the family. These were Missionary Joseph W.T. Turpin, his brother, Archdeacon Edmund Turpin, (my great grandfather), the Reverend George Grant, (Edmund's father-in-law) and Canon Milton E. Turpin, (my maternal grandfather). The only member of our family who developed a serious interest in religion was my son David, who studied Theology at Aberdeen University and graduated from there with a B.Th. in 2005. He was unable to further his career, sadly, as he suffered from chronic bipolar disorder and died by suicide in November 2008 at the age of 43.

In 2009, I compiled and published a book of poetry written by my son David A E Murdoch called "Flying My Own Plane" as well as a work entitled "The Final Solution to the Problem of Evil". Chipmunka Publishing, the mental health charity, owned by Jason Peglar of London, published both these books and they are available to buy in eBook form as well as paperback, from Amazon and the Chipmunka publisher's website.

I am a Christian myself and attend the local Presbyterian church in Tarves near where I live. My parents were regular church attenders. My mother and some of her family had a deep faith, which I believe helped to take them through some very sad and trying times. I am thankful that I was able to find comfort in my Christian faith, which I believe could be in my DNA to a certain extent, especially when it helped me to cope with the tragedy of my son's suicide.

This book is my first experience of being an author in my own right. My experience of writing to date has been of a very different genre and has almost entirely come from my work as a social worker. I have been lucky to have advice and help from the graduates who are amongst my family and friends.

# Introduction

For the purposes of clarity, when writing of colonial times, I shall refer to the country now called Guyana by its former name "British Guiana".

Ancestry.com LLC often referred to as "Ancestry", is an American genealogy company to which I have subscribed. I have gained access to relevant resources through both their web site ancestry.com and additionally their UK subsidiary, ancestry.co.uk. I shall be referring to these names interchangeably throughout the book.

I am also a member of the free FamilySearch Genealogy group which is provided by the Church of Jesus Christ and Latter-Day Saints. This can be a helpful site and does not require its members to belong to that faith.

I believe the details in this book are as true as they can be given that there were no birth records available in Barbados before the 19th Century. However, perhaps in the future, further information will be discovered which may substantiate or throw into question some of the details which I believe to be true at the time of writing.

# Section 1
# From Barbados and Guyana

# Chapter 1 - Who was Joseph Turpin?

**"Who was Joseph Turpin?" "A Secret in the Family"**

My father was "born and bred" in Scotland. My mother? Who was she?

My mother's maiden name was Turpin and I had always been aware that her paternal ancestors came from Barbados. Over the years, while growing up, Mum told me that her grandfather Edmund Adolphus Turpin, after qualifying as an Anglican priest at Codrington College, Barbados, had moved to Tobago to become a Canon in the Anglican Church there. He later moved to St Vincent and the Grenadines, where he ultimately became the Archdeacon of St George's Cathedral, Kingstown. Mum gave me a tattered photo of a baptismal font engraved with the words "The Venerable E. A. Turpin". She also told me that she and other family members thought his father, Joseph, could have been Bishop of Tobago.

Mum's claim that my great great grandfather, Joseph Turpin, had been a bishop was made more convincing when I read an online blog entitled "A Brief History of Charlotteville, Tobago" by Steve Sallfield. It was published online in 2013. Steve has given me permission to quote from his article:

"*In 1865, 27 years after the abolition of slavery, the two principal sugar estates in the north of Tobago were the 1800 acre "Charlotteville Estate" and the much smaller 150 acre "Pirates' Bay Estate". In 1865 both estates were acquired by Joseph Turpin, the Anglican Bishop of St Vincent. (PT). Joseph remained in St Vincent. Joseph's son Adolphus (Edmond) became Anglican Bishop of Tobago.*"

The information had been provided by my mother's second cousin Charles Turpin's wife Patricia Turpin who still lives in Tobago. She would have been given the information by her in-laws, my mother's first cousin Charles and his wife Mavis.

Armed with this information I set out on my quest to find "Joseph Turpin, Bishop of St. Vincent" and to try to discover how my mother's family came to be in Barbados.

# From Barbados to Banffshire

Mum died after a series of strokes robbed her of her ability to communicate meaningfully between 2004 and her death in 2008.

Dave and I spent three weeks in St Vincent and the Grenadines in January 2014. I decided to find out about Joseph Turpin, thinking that since his son had been the Archdeacon of St George's Cathedral there, he, Joseph, would also have been known of in St Vincent.

We visited the Kingstown Archives but there was no mention of Joseph Turpin in any of the documents we were given to read. However, there were a few references for my great grandfather, his son, Edmund, the Archdeacon, officiating at Church meetings. All quite dull stuff, such as how many sheep or cattle had been arriving or departing the islands. I was puzzled. Why was there nothing about his father? However, while we were in the archives, I did ask the archivist present if she knew anything about Joseph Turpin. The archivist seemed amused and told us that, coincidentally, the Archdeacon of a neighbouring island, had visited the archives the previous week, and had told her of his visit to St. George's Cathedral. He told her that when he asked a very elderly parishioner if the lady on the stained-glass window in the Cathedral was the Virgin Mary, the answer he received was *"No, she was Joseph Turpin's wife."* The archivist was amazed to see me coming into the archives so soon afterwards, asking about Joseph Turpin when she had never heard his name before that incident. She even called that Archdeacon on the phone and asked him to repeat the story to me, which he did. I was at first highly amused but then thought that it made perfect sense that a Bishop could have been able to honour his wife in that way.

In August 2017, during a visit to my cousin Lois in San Francisco, she told me that a DNA test she had taken recently revealed some African ancestry. She had been surprised by this. I told her that I had met with our cousin Timothy Ince and his wife Eileen in 2014. They had found through researching the name Turpin in the London Archives, that an 18-month-old boy called Joseph, born in 1815, son of a Black servant girl called Kate, was owned by a Timothy Turpin in Barbados. It seemed plausible though not conclusive, that

# Chapter 1 - Who was Joseph Turpin?

this Joseph could be our ancestor. Nobody had said that Bishops could not be Black.

Lois and I both agreed that our mothers may not have known of this, but that if they did, they would have kept quiet about it, such was the blatant racism of their era.

My cousin Timothy has told me since that time that his mother Sheila did tell him and his brother, when they were teenagers, that there was some Black ancestry in the family.

On my return home from the USA, I had my own DNA tested through Ancestry.com. I joined the Barbados Genealogy page on Facebook and their expert genealogist Sandra Taitt-Eaddy became interested in my story. I told her what my cousin Timothy had discovered and that I was certain that I knew who my ancestor was, but she was sceptical.

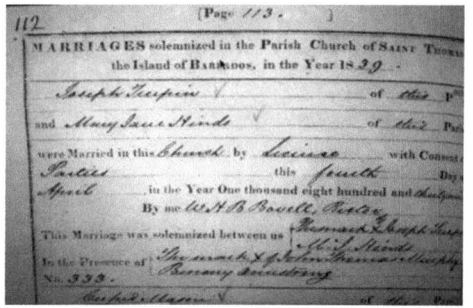

**Mary and Joseph's Marriage Certificate** The marriage certificate, sent by Ancestry.com, showed that while the bride, Mary Jane, signed her name, the groom, Joseph, marked his name with a cross.

This signified to me that he was illiterate. According to the Anglican Church baptismal records, my great grandfather, Edmund Adolphus Turpin was the son of this couple. Another nine children were also registered as having been their children. The marriage and the baptisms had taken place at Holy Innocent's Church, St Thomas, Barbados.

Sandra Taitt-Eaddy had been helpfully sending me information about a man she thought might be my ancestor. She had found two boys, William and Joseph, registered as having been enslaved on a plantation called New Castle in the parish of Christ Church, Barbados. It was owned by Thomas Best who employed a William Turpin as his Attorney or Plantation Manager. There was also an enslaved servant called Rebecca, described as "mulatto", who

9

# From Barbados to Banffshire

appeared consistently on the same slave registers as the two boys did. Sandra thought that this lady could be William and Joseph's mother. According to the Anglican Church register of baptisms for people owned by Thomas Best, Joseph, William, and Rebecca, along with several other enslaved persons were baptised on the same day in 1807. It is likely that the boys were born earlier than that as, in the record, they are described as child slaves and infants were not generally referred to as slaves. Sandra told me that it was customary practice for children to be baptised in a group for the convenience of their owner.

It is possible to track these boys from boyhood to adulthood through the Slave Registers. According to the 1821 Slave Register, Joseph Turpin was described as a "coloured" artisan who was 17 years old. Therefore, that would make Joseph's year of birth to have been 1803 or 1804. On studying William's burial record, it appears that he died in 1856 at the age of 60, placing his year of birth circa 1796.

Rebecca's burial record puts her as having died in 1869 at the age of 84. If this is correct her year of birth would have been circa 1785 which would surely rule her out of being William's biological mother as she would have only been 11 years old at the time of his birth. Rebecca could have been Joseph's mother as she would have been 18 or 19 at the time of his birth. William was therefore about 8 years older than Joseph but with both boys assuming the name Turpin, we can deduce that William Turpin, the plantation manager at New Castle was father to both the boys.

Towards the end of 2019, Dave and I decided to visit Barbados for a holiday and to do some research ourselves. Sandra had given me contact details for Professor Emeritus (History) Sir Woodville Marshall of the University of the West Indies. When we telephoned him, he invited us to his house which was on an elevated site, above the Black Rock Archives, with a lovely sea view overlooking the capital Bridgetown in the distance. We sat at a table in his open plan kitchen with veranda doors open to the garden. Small birds would come in and hop onto the table as we spoke. Woodville Marshall was a very approachable, kind man who seemed pleased to share his knowledge with us. He did accept that the Joseph I had

# Chapter 1 - Who was Joseph Turpin?

come across, owned by Timothy Turpin, could be my ancestor, and I may still find evidence that he had been a bishop. The one he was interested in, however, was the Joseph Turpin who, together with a man who might be his older half brother, William Turpin, had been instrumental in setting up the free village of Bridgefield.

The Joseph Turpin whom Professor Marshall knew about had never left Barbados. After emancipation in 1838, he had continued to work with his half brother William, at the Mount Wilton Plantation in Barbados, before moving to Bridgefield. Sir Woodville described both men as artisan carpenters. I left his house feeling quite disappointed that I still did not really know for certain who my ancestor was. I had expected to find Bishop Joseph Turpin, of course.

We visited the Holy Innocent's Church in the parish of St Thomas, where my great grandfather Edmund as well as all his siblings had been baptised. Their parents had been married there too. A helpful cleric showed us round the newly built church which had replaced the original building and told us about its history. I asked him if he had any idea why none of my Anglican clergy ancestors appeared to have worked, for any length of time, in Barbados. He said that the Anglican Church in Barbados at that time, preferred to employ white clergy of purely British descent to any rank higher than cleric. They were very particular about this, and potential priests had to provide proof of their ethnicity on their applications for employment.

This man had certainly never heard of a Bishop Joseph Turpin. Furthermore, there was nothing in the records to suggest that Joseph, father of Edmund, was ever a preacher, never mind a bishop, or that he had at any time in his life left Barbados. His name was not listed as having attended Codrington College where all Anglican trainee preachers had to go to study for the priesthood. The idea that my mother's great grandfather Joseph Turpin was indeed Joseph, the "coloured" carpenter, was now a strong possibility. However, I was not yet ready to let go of the myth that was Bishop Joseph Turpin.

# From Barbados to Banffshire

Finding Woodville Marshall's story about the free villages very interesting, we decided to visit these villages while we were in Barbados. We saw Rock Hall first. When there, we took photos of the very impressive memorial statue and vividly coloured mural (see the cover of this book). We did not find any memorial in Bridgefield. We later learned from the Professor that no such memorial exists for Bridgefield, the sister village to Rock Hall.

**Chattel House in Rock Hall**

We took this photo of one of the oldest houses in Rock Hall. It is a chattel house typical of those built by the enslaved to live in. These houses were built so that they could be dismantled and moved to another plantation. Joseph and William would have built similar houses in Bridgefield.

# Chapter 1 - Who was Joseph Turpin?

The following information was sent to me by Sandra Taitt-Eaddy. It includes a quote from an article written by Professor Woodville Marshall. She had alluded to the story before, but I had dismissed it as unlikely to have concerned any of my ancestors.

## The Ellcock Story

*"Reynold Alleyne Ellcock was murdered. His throat was cut. Three of his enslaved were accused and one man from a neighbouring plantation who it was said they paid to kill Mr. Ellcock. Upon Ellcock's death it was learned that he had made provisions in his will for every one of his enslaved who were classed as labouring adults to receive a 5 pounds annual payment. Of course, his relatives protested but the enslaved prevailed and in 1840 they got their money computed over the years since 1821 when the bequest was made known."*

Sandra added *"Your ancestors benefited from that bequest. My grandmother told me they used to call Rock Hall, "cutthroat village". It was a well-known story".* Sandra later told me that she had heard it said that Bridgefield was sometimes called "Blood field".

Towards the end of 2020 and after searching in vain for a Bishop Joseph Turpin, I had to accept that my ancestor, Joseph Turpin, had almost certainly been the enslaved artisan carpenter I had learned about from Sandra and Professor Marshall. I decided to contact Sir Woodville again and tell him that I was now very interested in the Joseph Turpin he had been telling me about. I was no longer looking for a Bishop Joseph Turpin who clearly had never existed. (See Appendix 1).

This was his reply to my email:

*"Of course, I remember you, mainly because my research on the Ellcock Bequest and the foundation of two villages in the parish of St. Thomas remains important to me. Let me make it plain that I have not been researching Joseph Turpin. I have been mainly concerned with how the Ellcock bequest was used, particularly its*

# From Barbados to Banffshire

*importance to the foundation of the villages of Rock Hall and Bridgefield.*

*I have a little information on Joseph Turpin because he was one of the recipients of the Ellcock Bequest and because he participated in the foundation of the Bridgefield village. Let me summarize what I have:*

*1. According to the 1821 Slave Register, Joseph Turpin was enslaved on the Mount Wilton plantation. He was described as a "coloured" artisan (carpenter) who was 17 years old.*

*2. In July 1840 he was one of the 83 formerly enslaved persons who received 85 pounds as a portion of the Ellcock Bequest. (Ellcock had owned the Mount Wilton plantation and in his 1820 will he directed that each "adult slave" should annually receive five pounds. He was murdered by a few of the enslaved in 1821).*

*3. Joseph Turpin was one of a party of twelve, led by William Turpin, possibly his brother, who left the Mount Wilton plantation in 1840, using their bequest to buy about 12 acres of land near the Social Hall plantation to establish the village that became known as Bridgefield. Joseph Turpin bought one and a half acres in the new village.*

*4. In April 1858, Joseph Turpin, who was evidently prospering as a carpenter and small farmer, bought his own small property, almost nine acres, which was half of a property called ALLEYNE/ALLEN VIEW (in the parish of St. Thomas).*

*5. Joseph Turpin made his will in August 1881 in which he named his children and some grandchildren and directed how his estate should be disposed of. He named two "natural" sons, THOMAS TURPIN, and THOMAS OSBOURNE TURPIN. His legitimate children were identified as: JOSEPH WILLIAM THOMAS, ANNA EMPHASIA, MALVINA, ALBERT AUGUST, EDMUND ADOLPHUS, FRANCES MARIA JANE, and GEORGE EYRE.*

*I hope that this is useful.*

*Woodville Marshall".*

# Chapter 1 - Who was Joseph Turpin?

The name **Edmund Adolphus** screamed out at me!

This was all I needed to be convinced we had conclusive confirmation that we had found Joseph Turpin, my direct ancestor. My "Eureka" moment!! The most important missing jigsaw piece was there. It was a great feeling.

I have not found further details on the two "natural sons", both called Thomas. They have not appeared in any lists from Ancestry.com or Family Search. Following their baptisms, the daughters named in Joseph's will do not appear anywhere else either. Perhaps they pre-deceased their father.

Sir Woodville has written a detailed history of the Ellcock story in which he tells us that there are mixed reports about what sort of man Mr Ellcock would have been. There are reports of him raping women on the plantation but also having same-sex relationships with men.

The story goes that he required a personal servant to share his bedroom and another man servant to sleep outside his bedroom door to protect him from attack. He had made the mistake of telling one of these men, his most trusted servant, while very drunk, that he had decided to leave his money to those enslaved who were classed as labouring adults at the time of his death.

The manservant was not happy about this as, in a previous conversation, Ellcock had said he was going to grant the servant his freedom very soon, and that he would not have to wait until Ellcock had died. The aggrieved manservant hatched a plot with some others to hire a man from another plantation to kill Mr Ellcock at the young age of 32. The family contested the will, so it was not settled until 1840. The court found the men guilty of the murder, and they were executed. They were hung, beheaded and their heads displayed on poles throughout the Plantation. A very gruesome story, but I now realise from having read "Sugar in the Blood" by Andrea Stuart, that this practice was not previously unheard of in Barbados, and for crimes not even as bad as that.

# From Barbados to Banffshire

The trial is detailed in Sir Woodville Marshall's article, "Rock Hall, St. Thomas: A Free Village in Barbados" in the Journal of Caribbean History 41:1&2 (2007):

*"Nothing in the official proceedings of the trial of the four slaves points to the existence of a general conspiracy or even of a conspiracy among the twelve or thirteen domestic slaves. In their confessions, the four accused - Billy-Prince, the hired hit man, Jack-Grig, a driver at Mount Wilton, James, and Jeffrey, Ellcock's personal servants and probable paramours - implicated each other in the murder. However, two of them, Billy-Prince and Jack-Grig, did indicate that the only other party to the conspiracy was Rita (Rittah), a twenty-nine-year-old domestic slave, who, according to them, had selected Billy-Prince as the hit man, presumably because he had a local reputation as a priest or obeah man, and had paid him a dollar to kill Ellcock. Surprisingly, Rita was not charged, not even with conspiracy, and she lived to eventually collect a share of Ellcock's bequest. One can only speculate that she informed on the conspirators to escape punishment."*

## Who was Rebecca? Was she Joseph's Mother?

Of all the people in this saga, for me, Rebecca must be the most interesting and I do wish I were able to find out more about her. The birth origins of the enslaved were cloaked in secrecy, especially for those like Rebecca who were described as "mulatto". The term is considered now to be offensive and is only used in a historical context. It usually means that the mother was Black and the father White. Who was her father? Why did she have the name Best? What sort of life did she endure? There are some encouraging facts such as that, in most of the slave registers with Joseph and William named, she is there too.

Another important indication that she was likely to have been Joseph's mother is the fact that, on her burial notice, she is named as Rebecca Best Turpin. Rebecca, William, and Joseph all took the Turpin name on emancipation, about 1837. However, William Turpin the putative father of both boys had long since died in 1820.

# Chapter 1 - Who was Joseph Turpin?

I just wonder how many other children Rebecca had to have. Did she have to suffer multiple rape which was the fate of many enslaved women on the Plantations? Or was she one of the more "favoured" servants? We will never know. The burial notice sent to me by Sandra states she died in 1869 at 84 years old. This information leads me to believe that we have the only confirmation of her identity we are likely to get. Records do show that Joseph was with her during his childhood.

**Burial Notice - Rebecca Best Turpin**

I have recently discovered the following post from historian Robert Morris on the Barbados genealogy group on Facebook. It is quite astounding and does throw some light on the identity of Thomas Best who owned Rebecca, William and Joseph.

*"Thomas Best is one of the most fascinating planters. Educated at Magdalen College, Oxford, he married Lady Emily Stratford, daughter of the Earl of Alborough. He killed Thomas Pitt in a duel. He and his wife had a sensational divorce and he returned to Barbados. He owned Moonshine Hall, Newcastle (Paragon), and Fairy Valley. His children were John Stratford Best who married Gorgeana Halliday, and Gorgeana Best who married Lord Tollemache. John Stratford Best died in England in 1888. I have no information on that branch of the family after. The Bests were known to have had coloured children, and there are rumours of a Thomas Best of Ridge and Frere pilgrim who had over 100 children!!!"*

# From Barbados to Banffshire

I had begun to suspect that Thomas Best may have been Rebecca's father, but further information found on UCL Centre for the Study of the Legacies of British Slavery, details that when Thomas died in 1829, he was only 48. Therefore, he would have been four years old when Rebecca was born. I am now considering the possibility that John Best, the previous owner of New Castle Plantation and father of Thomas Best may have been Rebecca's father. He owned the plantation she was born on before it was passed on to his son Thomas (see Appendix 7).

## Who was William Turpin?

William Turpin was the attorney or manager of the sugar plantation owned by Thomas Best around the time of William and Joseph's birth. According to the slave ownership records, he must have taken ownership of Rebecca, William and Joseph from Thomas Best at some point. There is a record of young William and Joseph, as well as Rebecca having been sold from New Castle, Christ Church by William Turpin to Reynold Alleyne Ellcock of Mount Wilton. Sandra considered he could have done this because William may have known that he was dying. He died in Christ Church, Barbados when Joseph would have been still quite young.

According to Ancestry records William Turpin married Sarah Price in Christ Church on 14th December 1814. In 1815 they had a daughter together called Sarah Margaret. Sarah Margaret is the only child named in William Turpin's will dated 13th July 1820. He instructed that, on his death, all his property should be equally shared by his children when the youngest reached the age 15. The one exception to this was Sarah Margaret who was to receive her portion as soon as she married "a good and virtuous man". I am grateful to Sir Woodville's research assistant who obtained the information for me. It must have been disappointing for William and Joseph not to be named in the will as his children. I am disappointed for them. Hopefully William Turpin did tell them he was their father before he died and gave them permission to use the name Turpin on the date of Emancipation, which is what they did. We have to be aware that in 1820, white plantation managers or owners were not encouraged to publicly declare they had fathered

# Chapter 1 - Who was Joseph Turpin?

any of their enslaved. Indeed, he had already sold them to Reynold Ellcock before he died. Perhaps it was a twist of fate that he did this as it resulted in the two boys being included in the legacy left to those who were enslaved on Mount Wilton Plantation and owned by Ellcock.

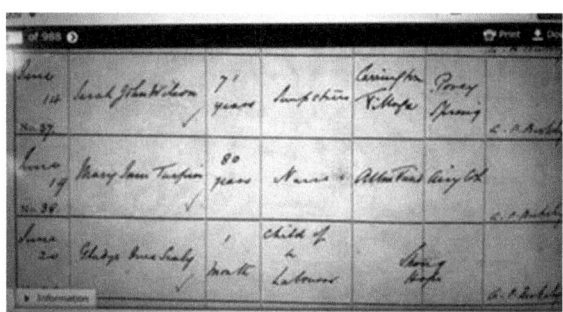

**Burial Notice of Mary Jane Turpin**

## Who was Mary Jane Hinds/Turpin?

According to the burial record for Joseph's wife Mary Jane Turpin, she was a nurse who died in 1896, in Alleyne View where she had lived with her husband and family.

Sandra has sent me information which would suggest that Mary could have been connected to the Anglican church in some way. Sandra wrote *"Your family's connection to the Anglican Church hierarchy is no coincidence. The Hinds name could have come from a planter called Edward Lake Hinds and his wife Mary Elizabeth. There is no birth certificate for Mary Jane so she may have been "an outside child" or formerly enslaved to the Hinds family."*

Was Mary Jane of Irish descent as had been suggested by some of my Irish relatives who live in Northern Ireland? Were the family escaping the Irish Potato Famine as my mother had mentioned to me whenever I asked? I have not found any record which would corroborate that assumption as the dates are wrong. However, a considerable number of Irish Catholics were sent to Barbados as indentured servants from the days of James 1st (see "The Irish Slaves" and "To Hell or Barbados" in the Bibliography).

# From Barbados to Banffshire

I hope she was not descended from these cruelly treated people. According to my April 2022 DNA Analysis (see Appendix 4) I have Irish ethnicity of 4% which I am thinking may have come through the line of Mary Jane Hinds.

Sandra also sent me this: *"Edward Lake Hinds owned land near to where Mary Jane lived at Airy Cottage, a property adjacent to Irish Town Plantation in Barbados. The church connection could have come from Edward Lake Hind's wife who was the daughter of a Reverend Jacob Lewis."* Was the close proximity of the area known as "Irish Town" just a coincidence?

Sandra has sent me some clearer evidence of Mary Jane's religion. She was a member of the Moravian Church in St Thomas Barbados (see Appendix 6). Her name appears in their baptismal record as a sponsor or godparent to two children related to Sandra as well as a number of other Black children. This leads me to wonder if she herself was mixed race. However, my DNA result does not back up this theory. This quote is taken from the Sharon Moravian Church website:

*"The impetus for the expansion of the Moravian Church in the Caribbean was a burning desire to take the Gospel of Jesus Christ to all oppressed peoples. Genuine Christian concern motivated these missions. In addition to preaching the gospel, the Moravian Church was active in providing an education for the slaves. It was one of the first organized religious bodies to establish primary and secondary schools for slaves in the West Indies."*

I wonder if Mary Jane was active in obtaining education for her children as well as others through her church. She could have been the influence for her two older sons to become preachers themselves.

It is worth noting the following information, which was provided by Sandra some time ago to help me find some of Mary Jane's possible history. It was taken from Woodville Marshall's book entitled "Of Halls, Hills and Holes: Place Names of Barbados".

# Chapter 1 - Who was Joseph Turpin?

*"Allenview, old site of small property, freehold village, is the eastern section of Welchman Hall Village. This section of the extended Welchman Hall village. It was formed on the half portion of the 17-acre Alleyne View property which in 1858 Joseph Turpin bought from Henry John Williams, Sarah Alleyne, and Mary Elizabeth Lake Hinds. The other half portion of the property was absorbed by the Sturges Plantation. In 1875, the village may already have been in formation, because Joseph Turpin owned "Allen View", now just over five acres in extent, of which Charles Downes and John Patrick each owned one acre lots at the same location. Turpin's bequests in 1881 consolidated the development of the village. The name, rendered as "Alleyne View", can be found in the 1847 list of landowners and also in official documentation up to the 1930s. But "Allen View" can be found in Joseph Turpin's will of 1881, and that rendering of the name can be found in the 1946/46 Rate Book and in list of polling districts."*

In the present day, there is a road junction in the area within the parish of St. Thomas's still known as Allen View. This junction is commonly referred to as **Turpins Corner pictured left** and is close to the popular tourist attraction of Harrison's Cave.

Modern Barbados is a prosperous, beautiful island with a stable government. They are no longer part of the British Commonwealth having left in 2022.

I do feel immensely proud of my great great grandfather, Joseph Turpin. I would have loved to have met him.

# From Barbados to Banffshire

## Edmund Adolphus Turpin – Archdeacon. Born 11th February 1851 - Died 1st December 1918

My great grandfather, pictured left, was the second son of Joseph and Mary Jane Turpin of Mount Wilton Plantation, St Thomas, Barbados. He was born there and baptised in April 1851 in Holy Innocents Church, St Thomas, Barbados as were all his siblings. According to Ancestry records his parents were married there in April 1839.

Edmund did follow in the footsteps of his older brother Joseph William Thomas, who was 9 years his senior, and was enrolled in Codrington College, Barbados to be trained for the Anglican Church Ministry. While Joseph went to Codrington College in 1868 at the age of 24 and was registered as "a negro", no such reference to Edmund's ethnicity was made when he was registered as a student there in 1874 - 75.

After qualifying, Edmund worked as a cleric in Barbados, baptising his own children including my grandfather Milton. He moved across the sea to become a Canon in Tobago. He preached there from 1886 to 1892, when he travelled to St Vincent to perhaps replace who I now know was his brother Joseph when he went to Sierra Leone and Fallangia to become a missionary in West Africa.

Here are two further extracts from "A Brief History of Charlotteville Tobago" blog by Steve Sallfield which refers to Edmund's movements in seeking employment as an Anglican Minister.

# Chapter 2 Part 1 – Maternal Great Grandparents

*"In 1865, 27 years after the abolition of slavery, the two principal sugar estates in the north of Tobago were the 1800 acre "Charlotteville Estate" and the much smaller 150 acre "Pirates' Bay Estate."*

*"He (Edmund) bought the estates from his siblings and built a small house on the site of the present "Great House". The market for sugar was declining in the 1880's and his managers began converting the estate to mainly cocoa. By the early 1900's cocoa was the main crop. The ruins of the sugar mill and the later cocoa factory are visible near the junction of the Windward Road and the Northside Road as one enters the village and there is another just above the Campbleton beach."*

I don't know whether the money to buy the estates in Tobago was provided by their father Joseph Turpin, who had inherited money from his murdered slave owner, Mr Ellcock of Mount Wilton Plantation, or from some other source. Another theory suggested by Professor Sir Woodville Marshall, is that land was being almost given away in the Windward Islands after the abolition of slavery. I can imagine this could have been due to unavailability of free labour which must have affected the profit margins considerably.

I did discuss my great grandfather Edmund with my mother before she became unable to speak following a series of strokes, from 2004. She told me that he went to St Vincent to preach there and subsequently became the Archdeacon of St George's Cathedral. She was very proud of this fact.

**Visit to St Vincent and the Grenadines**

In 2013, 5 years after my mother's death in 2008, Dave and I started making plans to visit the beautiful islands of St Vincent and the Grenadines. Driven by my desire to find out more about my mother's ancestors, we were always interested in travelling to places which had a special interest for us, other than to "just be a tourist". We contacted the office of St George's Cathedral and told them of our plans to visit the islands in January 2014.

# From Barbados to Banffshire

We almost didn't get there because on Christmas Eve 2013 the Islands of St Vincent and the Grenadines were hit by severe storms and flooding. Homes and holiday complexes were washed away. We contacted St George's Cathedral by email, and they kept us informed of the extent of the disaster. We began to doubt whether we would get there but the storms did abate, and the clean-up was successful. We were delighted to get the go ahead from the Church Office to still visit.

On the 9th of January 2014 we flew from Glasgow to Barbados where we stopped for 5 hours. We then boarded a very small plane to Kingstown, St Vincent. We checked into the Paradise Hotel, a beach hotel on the outskirts of Kingstown. The standard of the accommodation was good, and the staff were helpful. We could walk from the bar of the hotel directly onto the beach where we sat and watched a small ghost crab emerge from its burrow in the sand and stand sentry. We were able to swim safely in the sea just outside the hotel. St Vincent and the Grenadines are now served by an International Airport which is big enough to accommodate large planes flying direct from some of the major airports in the world.

We took a winding hilly taxi journey on the second day of our arrival to the capital, Kingstown, and were dropped off at St George's Cathedral Diocese Offices. We had prearranged a meeting with Dean Patrick Mackintosh who made us feel welcome. The Dean showed us several very old large reference books containing baptismal records, displaying the signature E. A. Turpin. He had obviously taken the trouble to find them prior to our visit.

There were also signatures by Milton Eyre Turpin, my grandpa, on the same records, dated from December 2018 which was his father's date of death. He had worked there briefly, following his father's death.

# Chapter 2 Part 1 – Maternal Great Grandparents

When I showed the Dean the damaged photograph, which Mum had given me of the baptismal font, he recognised it instantly. He said, "*I know exactly what that is. You must come and see it now.*"

He seemed delighted to take us to the Cathedral, and proudly show us the beautiful font made of solid marble. I was thrilled to see the letters emblazoned on its plinth "**The Venerable E.A. Turpin**". **This is the photo we took.**

It had been erected in the cathedral on 1st December 1918 according to an online entry I read about the Cathedral, "*as a memorial to Archdeacon Turpin for his many years of service as a prelate and a member of the House of Assembly*". (Diocese of the Windward Islands)

The Dean invited us to attend a church service in the Cathedral on the following Sunday. We were offered the chance to attend the earlier service at 5.30am, but quickly decided the later one, at 7.30 would suit us better. Neither Dave nor I are early morning people!

A post which I read on the Barbados Genealogy page gives some interesting insights into the policies of the ruling Anglican Church during the period of enslavement. The reason for the very early 5.30am service followed by the 7.30am one is reminiscent of when, in the days immediately after the emancipation of the enslaved, the planter class would attend the early service and the people of colour the later service.

The unpalatable truth is that (as posted on the Barbados Genealogy group on Facebook); "*in the early days of the Anglican Church in Barbados, the church held the position that the enslaved did not have souls hence Christian teaching was withheld from them. The majority then of the population of Barbados did not attend church nor any other place of worship during the enslavement period. For*

# From Barbados to Banffshire

*over 200 years, Sunday was a day of worship for the planter class and "Market Day" or a day of work for the enslaved."*

It was encouraging to see that when we were there, St George's Cathedral was very well attended, especially by people of colour. However, these attitudes do not disappear completely, and the stain of slavery is still inherent in all these beautiful West Indian Islands. How can it not be?

During the service, I was introduced to the large congregation as "Christine Turpin", descendant of Archdeacon Turpin. The Dean asked me to stand up so that the congregation could see me. I felt very humbled as well as quite embarrassed, as we were very casually dressed compared to the congregation, some were dressed as if they were going to a wedding. It was an impressive service with several baptisms taking place. Dean Patrick's resonant bass voice boomed out across the packed cathedral, giving a sermon laden with "hellfire and brimstone".

This appeared to be directed to the parents of the children about to be baptised. He seemed to be accusing them of coming to church for that reason only and I was reminded of the situation in Scotland. After the congregation had been chastised, and all the babies had been baptised, members of the congregation celebrating a birthday that week were invited to come to the front to be given birthday

greetings by the Dean and the congregation. It seemed like a very joyous occasion.

After the service, we searched for **Archdeacon Edmund's gravestone**, which we discovered was enclosed in a white painted but rusty wrought iron fence. It was not easy to find as we did not realise that a separate enclosed area facing the cathedral was reserved for former Archdeacons and other such dignitaries. Once we had been told where to look it was quite easy.

# Chapter 2 Part 1 – Maternal Great Grandparents

The cathedral is a beautiful, impressive piece of architecture. I have since learned that, after being very badly damaged by a hurricane in 1780. it had to be rebuilt. The rebuilding was said to be inspired by iconic French buildings such as the Palace of Versailles. This was due to a significant French presence in the Island in the late 18th century. There is a lot of information on the history of the church online and several YouTube videos talking about the building and the influences in the architecture. The cathedral is, however, in a poor state of repair and there is a big drive on for donations to have it restored.

## Grant / Van Buren Family History

**Julia Maria Grant Turpin was born in St Vincent on 22nd September 1852. She died on 1st April 1926 in Trinidad.**

Edmund met and married Julia when he moved to St Vincent to take up the post of Canon there. I have not found their marriage record, but their first child, Guy Edmund was born in 1877 so I am assuming they were married around 1876. According to Ancestry records, Julia was the daughter of Reverend George Grant and Caroline Rogers Van Buren. Reverend George was born in 1813 in St Vincent and the Grenadines into what is believed to have been a very wealthy slave owning planter family. I have not been able to establish where Reverend George was a preacher.

Julia's grandfather was Major Charles Grant (1785-1828) who married Mary Ann Hasler (b.1790). My newly found 3rd cousin Sandra Gamble has been sharing her knowledge of the family history with me. She lives in Australia We think Julia's grandparents were quite an interesting couple as two months before the Major died, he sued Mary Ann for divorce due to her adultery. There is an entry on Ancestry.com detailing the disagreements over the divorce settlement.

Julia's father, George Grant is registered on Ancestry.com as having died in Kensington, London in 1856 at the age of 43 when Julia would have been only 4 years old. I was not sure why he died in England, but Sandra Gamble while researching the Grants has

# From Barbados to Banffshire

found that Reverend George Grant had another family in England who share our DNA before he married Caroline in St Vincent in 1839. Another story perhaps worthy of further research.

Julia's brother George was born in 1850 in St Vincent and died there on 7th May 1902. Her brother Charles was born in April 1856 but I do not have a date or place of death for him. I have learned that La Soufriere, the volcano on St Vincent, which recently erupted in 2021, was believed to have taken the lives of George and some of his relatives when it erupted in 1902 killing 1,680 people in total. Fortunately, there have been no deaths due to the 2021 eruption, but the volcano did cause a huge amount of damage to crops and animals.

## The Mystery of the Lady on the Stained-Glass Window

When we visited the Archives in St Vincent in 2014, we were told that "Joseph Turpin's wife" was the lady on the stained-glass window in St Georges Cathedral but I could not understand how this could be the case: especially once I realised, she had not been a "bishop's wife". I decided to ask Sir Woodville Marshall if he could help solve the mystery. He said he knew one of his former students lived in St Vincent and kindly offered to contact him. The student, Adrian Fraser, contacted me directly, to say that according to former Dean, Ulric Smith, the lady on the stained-glass window is in fact "Archdeacon Turpin's wife". Mystery solved. My great grandmother Julia Maria Grant Turpin is therefore that lady (see colour photo insert).

The stained-glass window is of an impressive size filling the north transept of the cathedral. To give some context to its size, a story we were told when we were there, relates to the equally large stained-glass window in the south transept. This window depicts an angel dressed in a red cloak. The window was commissioned by Queen Victoria for St Paul's Cathedral but when she saw it, she rejected it for the colour of the cloak being "too catholic". The Bishop for St Vincent, discovering it while visiting St Paul's, arranged to take the window and have it transported to St George's.

# Chapter 2 Part 1 – Maternal Great Grandparents

Julia's mother, Caroline Rogers Van Buren (my great great grandmother) was born in 1821 in Tortola, British Virgin Islands. Caroline's father was John James Henry Van Buren, and her mother was Deborah Arrindell Ruan. Caroline died in St Vincent in 1899 at the age of 78. John James, her father, was born in Flatbush, Long Island, New York in 1788 and died in Port of Spain, Trinidad in 1858 at the age of 69 years. He was a major slave owner in the U.S. and according to Ancestry.com appears to have married several women. Perhaps he was a member of the Mormon church. The Van Burens can be traced back to before the 18th Century on Ancestry.com. They were originally a Dutch family. John James is from the same line as the former US President, Martin Van Buren. They were contemporaries and according to FamilySearch would have been distant cousins.

There are a number of girls named in the Ancestry registers as having been daughters of Caroline and George. Apart from one named as Emma Louise, possibly their first born, whose birth and death are given as 1840, there are no dates of death for Sarah Louisa and Catherine Emily. Perhaps these baby girls, like their sister Emma Louise, did not survive infancy either.

This family history is of particular interest to my sisters and I, as our sister, Betty, who died in 2018 expressed interest in the following photo of Julia's mother Caroline Roger Van Buren Grant and her family. Betty was diagnosed with Marfan syndrome as an adult. She also had diabetes since childhood. She studied the Marfan condition with interest, after her first baby died when only 10 days old. The doctors said the baby died of a congenital heart defect which could have been as a result of the genetic condition of Marfan syndrome.

The following photo was taken in 1850, probably before Caroline had been able to produce a child who survived beyond infancy. In the photo she looks like she could be carrying her as yet unborn son George, brother of Julia. He was born in 1850.

# From Barbados to Banffshire

**From left to right: Caroline Van Buren, her sisters Katy, Edith and her cousins of the Dunn family.**

Marfan syndrome features in extreme cases may include, tall and slender build and disproportionately long arms, legs and fingers. Betty has speculated that Katy resembles the pictures she had seen of a typical Marfan's person. Is it more than a coincidence that our great grandmother's family may have carried the Marfan's gene?

**There are some interesting facts about our Grant Family Ancestors.**

Julia's father George was a brother of Louisa Ann Grant, wife of Dr John Lister who inherited Shibden Hall, Halifax, Yorkshire from its famous owner, his cousin Anne Lister. Several books have been published about Anne Lister's extraordinary life. I am reading the one entitled "The Secret Diaries of Anne Lister" edited by Helena Whitbread, published in 1988. Sally Wainwright has written the television drama series "Gentleman Jack" which has been aired on the BBC. In the drama, Anne makes no secret of the fact that she is romantically attracted to women. It is a fascinating tale of a feisty charismatic woman who did a lot to preserve the historic 15th century building "Shibden Hall" in the state that it is today.

# Chapter 2 Part 1 – Maternal Great Grandparents

John Lister, oldest son of Julia Turpin's Aunt Louisa and Dr John Lister, inherited Shibden on the death of his father in 1867. John is therefore a distant relative of mine through my great grandmother Julia's line. He was 20 years old at the time and had attained an MA from Brasenose College, Oxford in 1867. John set up a school in 1877, after converting to the Roman Catholic Church, to teach impoverished young men a trade and help them gain employment. There were up to 200 students who benefitted from this.

John was a founder member of the Independent Labour Party and in the 1893 by election stood as the first Labour candidate for Halifax. Despite polling 3000 votes he did not win but became treasurer for the party and underwrote the ILP election campaign of 1895. Unsurprisingly, John went bankrupt due to spending all his money on charitable works and maintaining Shibden. He sold Shibden to his friend Arthur Selby Macrae. This man donated the grounds to Halifax, but John and his sister Anne were allowed to live there for the rest of their lives. This information is taken from the Shibden Hall visitor's guide published by Calderdale Council.

John, who was the last surviving member of the Lister family to occupy Shibden Hall found the now famous Anne Lister diaries which she had hidden at the back of her desk. There were over 200 volumes which detailed her travels as well as, unknown to him at the time, her sexual encounters with women. Before appreciating that the diaries were written in code, John decided to publish some of the plain handwritten extracts in the local paper in 1887. Later, John and his friend Arthur Burrell are reputed to have cracked the code which Anne used for the parts where she wanted to keep her sex life secret. Arthur Burrell recommended that John burn all 26 volumes of the sexual diaries as he considered them to be unpublishable, but John decided to neither publish nor destroy the diaries. He did not publish because he feared it would bring his own sexuality to the attention of the authorities as at that time homosexual acts were illegal. He hid the diaries behind a wall at Shibden where they remained until John died in 1933.

# From Barbados to Banffshire

Pictured left are my Great Grandmother Julia's Aunt Louisa and her husband Dr. John Lister. The portraits are displayed in the foyer of Shibden Hall.

Shibden is well worth visiting. It is a popular tourist attraction. The picture above is a photo we took when we visited in 2018. The grounds have been made into a tourist attraction with playpark, restaurant, boating lake and miniature railway but the building and its steadings have been preserved to be quite historically authentic.

**Shibden Hall**

# Chapter 2 Part 2 – Siblings of my Great Grandfather

## Joseph and Mary Jane Turpin had Ten Children

They are all listed in the Turpin Family details (See Appendix 10).

Of those ten children, apart from my great grandfather Edmund Adolphus, I have only been able to find out about their oldest daughter Sarah Jane and their oldest son Joseph William Thomas.

Sarah Jane was the first ancestor I was notified about when I joined Ancestry.com. I have been glad to befriend a fellow genealogy buff, her great grandson Bruce Coull who is my third cousin. He sent me the following profile of his great grandmother.

## Sarah Jane Turpin/Lind by her Great Grandson Bruce Coull

*"My maternal great-grandmother Sarah Jane Turpin, the first-born child of Joseph Turpin and Mary Jane Hinds, was baptized 13th August 1840 in the Parish Church of St Thomas, Barbados. On 21st August 1860 she married Alfred Bonthrone Lind at Holy Innocents Church, St. Thomas, Barbados.*

*Alfred Bonthrone 1841-1897 was born at Grant's Green, Manchester, Jamaica and came to Barbados before 1860. The Barbados Department of Archives marriage record states he was employed as a "clerk" and that he lived in St Michael's, and Sarah lived in Wilton Mountain, St Thomas, Barbados. Alfred Bonthrone's death date is based on the 1900 US census that states Sarah Jane is a widow who had been married 37 years. Sarah Jane and Alfred were the parents of 10 Lind children born between 1860 – 1879; four of them died in infancy.*

*Sarah Jane immigrated to New York City USA 25th September 1891 on the Ship Caribbee with 2 of her sons, Louis Alfred (1862-?) and Edmund Leonard (called Leonard) (1874-1958). Both theses*

# From Barbados to Banffshire

*sons are listed as living with her in Brooklyn New York in the 1892 New York State Census. The 1900 US census lists her living with sons Edmund Leonard (1874-1958) and Sinclair "St Clair" (1868-1909). Son Henry Lind (1869-?) immigrated to the US in 1888 before his mother and siblings. Of the 4 children of Sarah Jane and Alfred Bonthrone Lind who immigrated to the US, 3 of them had children born in the USA: Louis Alfred (1 child); Sinclair "St Clair" (3 children) and (Edmund) Leonard (8 children). Sarah Jane Turpin Lind died 6th October 1908 in Brooklyn New York and is buried in Greenview Cemetery in Brooklyn, New York USA.*

*Of my grandparents (Edmund) Leonard Lind/Ida Ester Burglund's children, my mother Ida Louise Lind (1924-1966) was the youngest of their eight children. In 1942 she married my father, Charles Coull (1917-1986) whose parents immigrated to the US from Scotland in 1909. Thus I, Bruce Charles Coull, have Scottish, Swedish (Grandmother Ida Burglund), English (Leonard Lind & Turpins) and 4% African genes via Lind family in Jamaica".   Bruce C. Coull*

**Joseph William Thomas Turpin was born on Mount Wilton Plantation, St Thomas, Barbados on 24th September 1842.**

Joseph, as well as his siblings were baptised in Holy Innocents Church, St. Thomas, Barbados. Some years ago, while browsing the internet and before I had begun to question my family ethnicity, I came across a letter written by a Joseph Turpin, Senior Missionary of the Pongas Mission in West Africa. I enjoyed reading it. My first thought was that I had found my great great grandfather Joseph Turpin who I believed had been an Anglican Bishop. But the date on the letter (1874) did not fit with him being the Joseph who was Edmund's father (I assumed that by that time; he would have been in his sixties at least). It was also stated that the Joseph Turpin who had authored the article was "of African descent". Given that I had never heard any mention of mixed ethnicity in the family, I sadly discounted the possibility that he could be my ancestor and put the thought to the back of my mind. I was disappointed because I had warmed to the author. I was excited to discover later in my genealogy journey that he was my great grandfather Edmund's

# Chapter 2 Part 2 – Siblings of my Great Grandfather

older brother. Joseph William Thomas Turpin was indeed the oldest son of Joseph and Mary Jane (Hinds) Turpin. He, along with his nine siblings, had been brought up on Mount Wilton sugar plantation, then moved to the free village of Bridgefield, in the parish of St Thomas, Barbados.

Joseph William and his siblings did not have to suffer the experience of being enslaved which their father, Joseph, Uncle William, and grandmother Rebecca had to endure.

Codrington College is the place in Barbados where Anglican clergy go to train for the priesthood. It was originally owned by a very wealthy plantation owner who left his estate to the Anglican Church. Christopher Codrington inherited two plantations at the age of 30 and left the estates to the Anglican Church in 1745. It was said to be "his dream".

Dave and I visited the college during our holiday in Barbados in December 2019. We were made very welcome by the staff there and were given tea and cakes. Later that afternoon, Principal or Dean of the college Dr Michael Clark met with us and gave us a tour of the college. It was very interesting. I think he may have been alerted to our presence by the cleric who had organised the refreshments. We took photos of the impressive college building and the beautiful grounds. We were also allowed to have a look through the records. The entry regarding Joseph William Thomas in the Codrington College register reads as follows:

**\*Turpin, Joseph William Thomas (negro) Ed. Cod.Coll;D 1868 Bar P.1871 S. Le S. Fotuba, Isle de Los 1867-72 Fallangia 1873-4 Fotuba 1867-77 Res (P264).**

The following is an excerpt from "The Mission Field" an Anglican Church publication which mentions Joseph's involvement in the Pongas Mission during his studies at Codrington College. The same publication details all the missionary work undertaken by the Anglican Church throughout the world.

# From Barbados to Banffshire

*"That the Barbados Board have made arrangements to send by the first vessel going direct from thence to Sierra Leone, two young men of African descent, who have been specially educated for the work in Codrington College, to supply the vacancies caused in the Mission staff by the resignation of Messrs. Maurice and Morgan. One of these, Mr. Turpin, has been for some time past ready to join the mission, and has been employed by the Archdeacon of Barbados as a Reader and Catechist amongst the Caribs in St. Vincent, under the direction of the Rev. Mr. Frederick, until the opportunity should offer of sending him to the Pongas. Writing from Domingia, 22 November 1866, Mr. Duport mentions that Fallangia was visited by a tornado on Sunday, 21st October, which seriously damaged the church and Mission premises."*

*"The reports of the Pongas Mission for the last quarter have been received by the English Secretary. They give an account of steady Mission- work both at Fallangia and Domingia. The smallpox was still prevalent at both stations, and the attendance at the schools had consequently fallen off, some of the boarders being still absent. The number of scholars were, at Fallangia 35, with an average attendance of 25, at Domingia 13, of whom 10 are in daily attendance. Mr. Macaulay, the newly appointed catechist of S. P. G. was with Mr. Duport at Fallangia, and Mr. Bickersteth at Domingia Messrs. Turpin and Doughlin, two students from Codrington College, had arrived. They have been licensed by the Bishop of Sierra Leone as catechists and are preparing for ordination. The Mission staff is now complete."*

The following link is to the article I found by Joseph William Thomas which is well worth taking the time to read. He makes several mentions of his sister who accompanied him on the mission but does not mention her by name:

http://anglicanhistory.org/africa/turpin_pongas1874.html?fbclid=IwA R2wp

36

# Chapter 2 Part 2 – Siblings of my Great Grandfather

**Pongas Mission circa 1874**

This is a photo of some of the people involved in the Pongas Mission in West Africa. I am thinking that Joseph may be the clergyman holding a baby, to the left of the woman wearing a hat. He does not name her, but I think she may have been his sister, Ann Euphrasia, who was two years younger than him. Not confirmed, just a guess. I hope I am not wrong with this assumption.

Below is an amusing excerpt from the article I have been referring to. I think it brings his personality to life for the reader who may not be able to access the article online:

*"While in Sierra Leone we paid a visit to the village of Regent, in the mountain district, where Mr. Williams, who was for a short time connected with our Mission, is pastor. The scenery was delightful, and the view of the garrison and harbour obtained from the hill was very good. The mode of travelling in Sierra Leone is either in Bath chairs or by means of the hammock. My sister was to be carried up in a hammock. This is simply a hammock suspended from a long pole, carried on the heads of two men. Having walked a little way, she entered this peculiar carriage. It was held to the ground, while she entered, and then, lying at full length with a pillow under the*

# From Barbados to Banffshire

*head, with a jerk it was raised to the shoulder, and with another to the heads of the men. At first starting there is a swinging motion, and it is really amusing to see the expression in the countenance of one unaccustomed to this mode of travelling, as the hands tightly grasp the sides, or vainly endeavor to reach the pole. In a short time, however, the swinging ceases, and the motion settles into a pleasant jolt, and the traveler chats, looks about, holds her umbrella, or reads, and has quite a comfortable appearance. On arriving at their destination, careless bearers will sometimes drop their burden rather unceremoniously on the ground, leaving the unfortunate occupant to scramble up as best she may. Men travel a little differently. Sitting astride, with feet resting in a pair of stirrups, book in hand and umbrella overhead, it does not at all seem an uncomfortable mode of getting on, though for my part I always prefer to be on my own feet." (The Pongas Mission, by Joseph Turpin (1874))*

According to Ancestry records, Joseph married Julia Rosamund Meyer in St Croix, Danish West Indies on 26th September 1877. This was only three years after the date on the article I have referred to above (The Pongas Mission). They had three children, Julia Chittendon Turpin, Winifred Josephine Turpin and Fred Turpin.

I have been in touch with a lady via Ancestry.com who has given me some other information, but she did not know that Rev Joseph was born and brought up in Barbados. She has asked a relative to try to do some further research on the family. **She also shared this photo of Julia, wife of Rev. Joseph to whom she is related.** I have not heard any further news from her.

# Chapter 2 Part 2 – Siblings of my Great Grandfather

Joseph is credited with having worked in St Vincent prior to travelling to West Africa. I had been disappointed that we were not given any information of a Joseph Turpin having preached in St Vincent when we were there in 2014. Joseph is believed to have died in Trinidad on 20th May 1903.

Regarding Steve Sallfield's blog which I quoted in Chapter 1, it is now clear that contrary to that information, Joseph William Thomas's father was an enslaved carpenter, Joseph himself was a Senior Missionary in West Africa and his brother Edmund was Archdeacon in St Vincent and the Grenadines. There were no Bishops in the family. After I had completed my research on Joseph senior's real identity as a carpenter and not a Bishop, I contacted Steve and told him of the errors. He agreed to change his document. To date this has not yet been done. More of Steve Sallfield's article is quoted in the chapter on Cyril Anderson Turpin. Cyril was my grandfather's third oldest brother, and he became the main owner of the Cocoa Plantation in Charlotteville which was first acquired by Reverend Joseph William Thomas Turpin.

Reverend Joseph was a most interesting person to write about. I wish I had been able to make his story more cohesive and not so dependent on snippets of other publications. I'm sure he could have written a very interesting book about his own experiences.

**Anglican Theological Codrington College
Parish of St. John, Barbados**

# From Barbados to Banffshire

**Canon Milton Eyre Turpin was born in Barbados on 14th August 1884**

My maternal grandfather was the fourth son of Edmund Adolphus and his wife Julia. My sisters and I knew him as Grandpa Turpin. He was baptised on 11th September 1884 in Barbados by his father Reverend Edmund Turpin who was Acting Curate there at the time. The address was given as Alleyne's Bay House, St. Thomas, Barbados. Alleyne was the area in which his grandparents Joseph and Mary Turpin had lived.

The family lived in Barbados while Edmund attended Codrington College where he trained for the Anglican Ministry. They moved to Tobago when Milton was two years old. He would have spent his early school years in Tobago. When the family moved to St Vincent, Grandpa would have attended school there from the age of eight, completing his education at Kingstown Grammar School. He graduated from Codrington College, Barbados in 1907 and, according to his Anglican Church resume (see Appendix 8), began his career as an Anglican Church Curate working around various charges in British Guiana and the West Indies.

Grandpa's first charge after qualifying was as Priest in Charge at the Bartica Mission from 1911-1917. While there from 1911-1912 he was also Acting Chaplain at the penal settlement on the Mazaruni River a tributary of the Essequibo. This must have been a stressful charge as his son Milton shared with me that his father had told him that he had to give last rites to those facing execution by hanging. He was particularly concerned with those people who did not have the mental ability to know why they were there or why a noose was being put round their necks. This troubled him and I'm sure he was glad to give this position up.

# Chapter 3 Part 1 – Maternal Grandparents

Grandpa married my grandmother Constance Margaret Clark Gray on 14th August 1914 and took his new bride to Bartica to live with him there. Bartica was quite a primitive place for a young woman, who was born and brought up in the city of Edinburgh (see story at end of Chapter 4 Part 2 "Guyana Holiday 1993"). Bartica is a small town on the Essequibo River, a 65 miles journey from Georgetown, the capital of Guyana. It is very remote even now. The best way to get there is by speed boat on the river.

Their first child, Grace Julia, was born in Bartica, and I have described the traumatic situation surrounding her very difficult birth in Grace's own story. Grace was born in 1915. The family moved to Barbados when Grandpa became the vicar of St Saviour's Church, St Andrews Parish, Barbados from 1917–1921. Daphne, Margot and Michael were all born there during that period.

In 1921 the family moved from Barbados to Berbice, British Guiana with their family of four very young children including Michael, the baby, who must have only been a few weeks old and Grace, a disabled child, the oldest at 6 years old. Grandpa became Rector of St Michael's, Fort Wellington which was where my mother and her siblings spent most of their childhood. While working in Fort Wellington as the vicar there, it appears, according to the Anglican

Church records, that he was required to continue to serve the Bartica Mission as Acting Priest in charge until 1931. It must have been difficult to get a vicar to go and work in the primitive Bartica mission. In 1931 he had taken on the job of Acting Vicar of Belladrum. Grandpa's final charge was St Saviour's Church in Georgetown.

**Here are Grandpa and Granny Turpin** with their three oldest daughters, **Grace** Julia Mary, Gertrude **Daphne,** and Constance **Margot** (my mother).

# From Barbados to Banffshire

Grandpa adored his daughters and gave them all pet names. He called Grace "Grace Darling", Daphne "Daffodil", and Margot was called "Marie Mar".

They were a very busy couple indeed. I think that Granny Turpin did have her older sister Mary La Frenais (Aunt Mamie) living nearby. I am assuming they would have had some servants to help with the children and household tasks.

There ensued a period of respite for Granny from having children after Michael was born in 1921. Christine Maude Eyre was born in 1925, Milton Everett Andrew in 1926 followed by a further period of respite from childbirth with their youngest child, Guy Oswald Garnet being born in September 1931.

During his time as an Anglican priest coping with dual roles in more than one church as well as father to seven children, Canon Turpin was fully occupied. Both my mother and her sister Christine used to say he was quite strict with them, and they were not allowed to interrupt him in his study when he was working on his sermons. Although he did appear to me to be very kind and approachable, he was a typical parent of the time and expected the best of behaviour from his children. Did the minister's children have to be perfect? Mum describes having fun and games with him such as cricket and picnics at Easter. Indeed, in her own words which are quoted in Chapter 4, she describes an idyllic childhood which does not seem to take account of how very busy her parents were when their children were young. Grandpa was also very strict with the girls when they started dating. They were not allowed to go out with a boyfriend on their own and had to have a chaperone, usually, a grown-up lady friend of their parents.

# Chapter 3 Part 1 – Maternal Grandparents

Constance Margaret Clark Gray was born at 17 Royal Park Terrace, Edinburgh on 27th February 1890.

My Grandmother Constance, known as Connie or Granny Turpin, is the lady on the far right next to my grandfather Canon Turpin.

The photo was taken at my parents wedding in April 1940. The bridesmaid on the left is Mum's sister Christine and the flower girls were Jennifer Castles and Eve Mowat, two children my mother taught as their governess. The man on the left was a family friend.

I do have a hazy recollection of Granny as a loving smiling lady, running towards me with open arms. Mum used to have a photo of her in an album. She had shiny black hair and beautiful skin and looked quite cuddly and plump. I have not been able to find that photo again.

**Peter Gray was born in Inverness on 17th September 1863.**

My maternal great grandfather was the second youngest son of James and Margaret Clark Gray. They lived at 35 Friars Street, Inverness. James Gray owned a roofing business in Inverness. Peter's brothers were William, Murdo and James.

Peter moved to Edinburgh after his marriage to Grace on 24th March 1887. Their children, including my grandmother, were all born in Edinburgh. At first, they lived at 17 Royal Park Terrace. Constance had two sisters, Mary (Aunt Mamie) born 1889 and

# From Barbados to Banffshire

Grace Christian (Aunt Chris) who was born in 1893 when the family moved to 2 Willowbrae Avenue. My sister Avril met her when she visited her in her home in Runcorn, Cheshire, with my mother in 1971. She recalls a small, pleasant lady with red hair. According to Ancestry records, Peter was promoted to Chief Journalist for the Edinburgh Evening News. He worked as a journalist until he died in 1900 at the age of thirty-seven. Cause of death on his death certificate was cirrhosis of the liver. Mum told us he had caught pneumonia while visiting London to report on Queen Victoria's deteriorating health. Her mother, Constance, had been told that this trip to London hastened his early death. It had been a very cold day and Peter had been in poor health. He died at his home in Willowbrae Avenue.

**Grace North Rowley was born in New Spynie, Morayshire, Scotland on 13th September 1868.**

My mother's grandmother Grace was the oldest daughter of Mary Fraser and William Rowley. Mary died in Elgin when Grace was only seven years old. Grace's father, William Rowley, was born in England in 1845. After Mary died, he met and married Annie Watson in December 1875 in Elgin. They had at least thirteen children so Grace, being the oldest daughter, would have been kept busy helping her stepmother to look after the children. She would have experienced grief and loss, throughout her childhood as records show that as well as losing her mother at the age of seven, at least five of her step siblings died in infancy.

After Grace's husband Peter's death, the family moved to 81 Trafalgar Lane, Leith where Grace died seven years later at the age of thirty-nine. Her two oldest daughters had already emigrated to British Guiana the previous year. Her death certificate states the cause of her death on 28th October 1907 at the age of 39 to be "death by hanging". I was shocked and saddened to receive this news via Ancestry.co.uk.

# Chapter 3 Part 1 – Maternal Grandparents

**Here is Grace's Portrait**. Such a sad looking beautiful lady. I have learned from Ancestry that her maternal grandfather also took his own life by hanging at the age of 48.

My mother never met her maternal grandparents, but I can remember her telling us that her grandmother "*died of a broken heart*". Her death must have been a terrible shock for Connie and her siblings. I wonder if Connie could have brought herself to tell her children how her mother had died.

Granny Turpin was only seventeen when this tragedy occurred and had already left Scotland the previous year to accompany her older sister Mamie on the voyage back to British Guiana. Aunt Mamie had married Doctor La Frenais and they had already settled in that country. Mamie returned to Edinburgh for a holiday in 1906. On the return journey she asked her sister to accompany her back to Guyana. Connie was only 16 at the time. She was to be a help to her sister in looking after their children. The children were Joe, Cissy (who married Claude Forsyth), Walter, Tim and Yvonne. These names used to pop into my mother's conversations about her family. Granny was to remain there until her marriage to Grandpa Turpin in 1914.

**Granny Turpin had one brother James Thomas (pictured on the left)** who was the youngest of the family and was born in 1895 at 2 Willowbrae Avenue, Edinburgh. His father died there when James was five years old. He would have been only 12 years old when his mother died.

Mum told us James was killed in the First World War. Military records confirm that he was killed in action in Flanders, France on 3rd August 1917. He was with the Queens

# From Barbados to Banffshire

Own Highlanders. His death was yet another heartbreak for our Granny to have to cope with so far from her home city of Edinburgh. She would have just given birth to her second daughter, Daphne, less than 2 months before this tragedy.

James's uncle, Arthur James Rowley, also fought in France. He was injured on the battlefield but died on the HMS Halcyon on 30th November 1918 at the age of 27. Arthur had an older brother Vincent who was also killed in the First World War in 1916.

My great grandfather Peter's brother James married Anne and they had 4 children. They took my grandmother, Connie, to live with them for about a year when she was 15 years old. Mum was therefore keen to become acquainted with the family as a link to her mother. Their oldest was Northey Gray who married Bunty. Mum looked forward to him dropping in to visit us at the farm. They did visit us at least once when I was at home, and they attended my first wedding in April 1964.

Northey and Bunty had a son, Hamish Gray, who married Judith, and became a Conservative MP for Ross and Cromarty (see article on Lord Gray in Appendix 9).

## Life in British Guiana

Mum told us that her mother Connie found it very difficult to cope with the heat and change of lifestyle from Scotland to the tropics. She had arrived in British Guiana in 1906 and within a year of her arrival was to receive the very tragic news of her mother's death in October 1907. I am sure Mamie and Connie would have been a comfort to each other at such a sad time. It must have been very difficult for them being so far from home. Their sister Christian and their brother James must have had to be looked after by their grandparents, William and Annie Rowley, as they were still quite young.

Connie was very popular with the parishioners. She was musically talented with a beautiful singing voice and would play the piano and

# Chapter 3 Part 1 – Maternal Grandparents

sing at the church concerts, encouraging her children to do the same. A regular "Von Trapp" family perhaps! Mum loved to reminisce about her and sing the songs her mother taught her.

Granny set an example of how to appear cheerful regardless of life's disappointments. My mother certainly seems to have absorbed this example and has passed it on to us as well. Bringing up her children and being the minister's wife did hopefully help to distract Granny from feeling too unhappy.

Further tragedy was to shatter Granny's happiness, when in 1933 she suffered the enforced departure of her daughter Grace. Grace was only 18 when she was taken to England for assessment and treatment because of her disability and strange behaviour (see Grace's own story in part two of this chapter). This was a bitter blow from which my grandparents never recovered. Connie did sail to England one year later to see Grace at the home of her sister Chris hoping to be allowed to take Grace back home with her; but this did not happen This must have been devastating for her as well as Grace. We learned from Uncle Milton, her second youngest son, that Granny sought solace through alcohol. He told us he remembered hearing both parents crying in the night for their "Gracie Grace". Granny Turpin died on 17th March 1949 of a heart attack, no doubt hastened by stress, loss, and the effects of alcoholism. She was 59.

Before Granny Turpin's death my grandparents were able to move from the very rundown vicarage they lived in, to a new bungalow in Hague Village, West Coast Demerara. Their daughter Daphne had been instrumental in finding the bungalow as she was concerned at how disabled with arthritis her father had become. Daphne fought hard to get the church to let them have the new bungalow.

Thanks to Elizabeth Alleyne for sending me a link to an article which I have quoted from below. It is a Guyanese newspaper article which includes quotes from musician Dave Martins' column, So It Go, in the Stabroek News edition of March 2010. It is available online.

# From Barbados to Banffshire

*"Hague is a small West Coast Demerara village located about 12 km from Vreed-en-Hoop. It was once a Dutch plantation and took its name from the capital of the Netherlands."*

The house described in the article as the *"Haunted House of Hague Village"* is none other than the house in which my grandparents lived and where Granny Turpin sadly died. Hopefully, these tales are indeed only local folklore and rumour.

A Guyanese musician of some repute, Dave Martins, who lived there for 20 years and is now 87 years old is quoted in the article as saying *"No haunted-house talk reached my ears, but it must have started, because in later years, when three other people died in that same house, one of them a pastor, the speculation became fact – "da house haunted, buddy" – and now it seems to have become part of our folklore. It is the way of such things that logic is often out the window."*

The following is an extract from an obituary sent to me by Tim Ince:

*"The funeral of Mrs. M.E. Turpin, wife of Canon M.E. Turpin, Vicar of the Anglican Churches on the West Coast took place on March 17. It was largely well attended.*
*Mrs Turpin was well known to the parishioners and by her genial disposition she had endeared herself to all. The corpse was removed from the house of mourning, Hague, followed by Canon Turpin and his youngest son Guy.*
*When the hearse arrived at St Simon's Dekinderen, the Sunday School choir sang "Loving Shepherd", and the body was borne into the church by the pall bearers. The body lay in state until 4pm when the Bishop of Guiana and the Archdeacons of Guiana and Demerara arrived. A choral service was conducted by the Bishop, the* Archdeacons *taking part, after which the interment was made in the church yard."*

# Chapter 3 Part 1 – Maternal Grandparents

Grandpa Turpin lived for another 12 years after the death of his wife and was supported by his sister Stella who often went to stay with him when he lived in the vicarage as well as after they moved to Hague Village. His youngest son Guy was also at home with him until he too left for the UK to seek employment in 1951. She mentions in letters that he suffered badly from arthritis in his knees and had great difficulty walking although he did continue to preach at St Saviour's Church in Georgetown. We noticed his disability when he came over to the UK in 1953 to visit us all. Milton, Michael and Guy were all in the UK by this time. We liked him very much. He was very interested in each one of us, and we warmed to him immediately.

Before he arrived, I remember Mum insisted we have ringlets put in our hair using strips of old white cotton sheet. This was to improve our appearance next day for Grandpa's visit. We all had straight hair which was not the fashion. They were most uncomfortable and difficult to sleep in. Mum would say cheerfully "*Pride feels no pain*". When he arrived, he came up the stairs to see us "sleeping". He exclaimed in horror, "*Why are the girls wearing bandages, Margot? Have they been in an accident?*" Next day we asked him to come with us to Rothiemay village which was a mile away from our farmhouse. We were oblivious to his pain as we skipped mercilessly down the road in front of him, looking back to see poor Grandpa hobbling down the road in the distance.

We were all extremely sad when we heard that Grandpa died on his journey home from his trip to the UK to visit us. He had developed acute appendicitis towards the end of his homeward journey to Demerara. The ship he sailed on was the "Colombie". He was taken off the ship at Bridgetown, Barbados to receive treatment in hospital there. Auntie Daphne flew from Jamaica to be at his bedside. She was very thankful to find that her Uncle Charles and Aunt Mavis had also made the journey from Tobago to offer support. "They were a great comfort to me", she said in her letter to my mother. The Doctor in Barbados told Daphne there was no hope of a recovery as peritonitis had already set in. Grandpa told Daphne that when he knew he had ruptured his appendix he appealed to the doctor on

# From Barbados to Banffshire

board the liner to operate on him as he knew that time was of the essence. The doctor refused to do this, and Grandpa had to disembark in Barbados to be taken to the hospital there on 7th September 1953. They were only able to provide him with antibiotics and painkillers. Auntie Daphne goes on to conclude in her letter that she held the doctor on the ship responsible for her father's death.

Grandpa died on 14th September 1953 of peritonitis followed by pneumonia, so he did not get home to Demerara. He was buried in St Leonards Church yard, Bridgetown, Barbados on 15th September 1953 below the windows to the west of the chancel. Bishop Gay of Barbados officiated at the funeral service. When Dave and I visited Barbados in 1989 we tried to find his grave accompanied by Mum's cousin Dulcie Warren. She had kindly given us free accommodation in her home in Worthing. We were eventually told by a cleric that the new church had been built over his grave and there was nothing to show for Grandpa having been buried there. He had never preached there. There was talk of the family clubbing together to have a commemorative plaque put on the Church wall somewhere, but as there were no close relatives living in the West Indies by that time, nothing was done about it sadly. Daphne's letter concluded with details of Grandpa's passport stating his profession to be "Clerk of the Holy Orders" and describing him as being 5ft 8in tall, with blue eyes and light brown hair.

I would like to share some excerpts from one of the letters written by Grandpa Turpin to his sister Stella while he was on holiday in Tobago with his brother Cyril. He refers to Cyril as "The Captain". "Dazzar" was his sister Stella's pet name for Grandpa. There are numerous letters between them, which give a flavour of Grandpa's personality as well as Cyril's later life. Cyril had become a heavy drinker. It is clear from the letter that their relationship was sometimes strained for various reasons. Although Grandpa does appear to have been the fitter of the two brothers, he predeceased Cyril by 4 years.

# Chapter 3 Part 1 – Maternal Grandparents

*"My Dear Stella,*
*I have pinched a sheet or two of the captain's paper out of his paper cupboard. If he only got to know, what a cussing I would get. A certain wind and rainstorm woke me up at 1.30 through the bathroom door slamming to with a bang and the wind pouring in through the upper half of the door which I have open at nights, as I find the room hot, and I like plenty of air. It is now raining fast and heavy, with thick black clouds all around the ridges of the hills and plenty of mist clinging and meandering down into the valleys. Conditions were just the same on an afternoon last week when rain fell steadily for over an hour accompanied by sharp flashes of lightening and roaring thunder. The captain was afraid his gasoline might catch a fire and burn up car and house. There are again this morning flashes of lightning followed by thunder."*
*"Yesterday I left the captain's house immediately after lunch and walked over to Pirate's Bay where I enjoyed a lovely swim and soak in the sea. The water was very salty. I left at 4. On the return journey, when I got to the village, I met Melville and Woodby, with their guns standing like two musketeers. They gave me the news that the captain had driven down to the beach by the Rest House and got into a boat with the motor engine attached, to go for a spin in the bay. For a long time, the engine would not start. Benjamin must have got a great deal of cussing off. I am glad I was not there for I would have been considered the Jonah. Eventually the engine started and when climbing the short cut to the house I saw the boat steam into Pirate's Bay. On a point in the short cut, I followed a wrong path taking me away from the house. I had to scrabble through no end of bush high up the hill until I found myself at the bottom end of the goat enclosure. By holding on to the wire I pulled myself alongside of it through bush to the top. On entering the path from there to the house, I got to the house and quietly went upstairs poured out myself a good shot of rum out of the captain' s bottle on the table, got an iced bottle of ginger ale from Leonora and bolted back downstairs. I had only drunk half my drink and changed my dripping wet shirt for my pyjamas jacket when the car drove up and the captain came in led by Benjamin lighting their way by candlelight."*

# From Barbados to Banffshire

*"On Monday, he came downstairs all unaided. on trembly knees and shuffling feet, played the piano, sang a while, and returned as he came. He did the same thing last week, Friday, after cussing up everybody, Leonora, Benjamin, the watchman and whoever rang the telephone. He says I am too ungainly in his sight with my big belly. He does not like to see a Turpin with such a big corporation. I eat too much. I should be out of doors travelling over the hills and valleys of the estate instead of sitting down in lazy fashion in the house. When it is fine, I go away from the place and keep out."*

*"Wednesday night I was alone in the house with him. The servants had gone home, and no watchman came up, about 9 o' clock at night I heard a funny clinking noise, coming to the conclusion he was trying to get somewhere, I went upstairs to find him sitting at the dining table with a huge spanner trying to unscrew the top of a large bottle of preserved fruit of plums saying he wanted fruit, not oranges, fig bananas, and he could find none. That you had used up all of his tin of preserved pears instead of using the avocado pears which he does not like. I opened the bottle and gave him a good helping of the plums, helping myself to a very small quantity. I remained up with him until 11 o' clock when he said he felt sleepy and would sleep in his chair, I left and came down. About 2.30 a.m. I was awakened to hear him shouting "Watchman Watchman! Leonora! Watchman!" I bolted upstairs to find him sitting up on the flat floor at the foot of the chair right between the door leading into the small bedroom and the dining table, facing the table. At once the challenge rang out "What are you doing here?" When I told him, I heard him shouting for the watchman, and knowing servants and watchmen were not in the house, I came too, to see what he wanted. He became civil then, and told me he was "dreaming he was going to Nairobi" and woke up to find himself in the posture he was in. He must have crawled from his bed along the floor where he was I said within myself "that's a good Baron Manchusson one". For little did he know that I had crept up the stairs halfway and saw him lying stretched at full length on the floor of his chair, stone and small foot bench pushed away and the cushion as his pillow before I got into bed. I did not touch him until he asked me to get him into a standing position. Gripping him under the arm, I managed to get him upright, though he was no mean weight to lift. He walked fairly*

# Chapter 3 Part 1 – Maternal Grandparents

*firmly through the pantry way, while I took up the lamp and lighted him into his room where a candle was burning on his table. Putting down the lamp, I got him into the bed, covered up his legs to the knees with his blanket, got him water with a bottle of ginger ale. It was 3 a.m. when I got back into bed. So that was that."*

*"I have done no fishing since you left. The men cannot leave cocoa picking to accompany me. I have not found your purse nor scissors so that's that". Right Now, I must close here with love to your Sheila & John. Yrs. Dazaar"*

**Author walking back from Pirates Bay to Charlotteville
Tobago 1989**

# From Barbados to Banffshire

## Grandpa Turpin's Siblings, the Children of Archdeacon Edmund and his wife Julia

**Guy Edmund Turpin was born on 22nd July 1877 in Barbados.**

My mother used to talk of her Uncle Guy, although he died before she was born. He became a surgeon and never married or had children. The story I remember Mum telling me about him was that he suffered a burst appendix and as there was no surgeon available to help him, he performed the operation on himself. He was living in Trinidad at the time. Although he was able to survive that ordeal, he died not long afterwards of Blackwater fever (a complication of malaria) in Scarborough Hospital, Tobago on 6th October 1912 at the age of 35.

**Ernest Albert Turpin was born on 12th January 1879 in Barbados**

Ernest also became a surgeon, studying in Edinburgh for his certificate to practise. After qualifying he practised in San Fernando, Trinidad where he was held in high esteem. After his death in 1923 a plaque was unveiled in his honour and has been placed on the wall of the Resident Surgeon's office facing the main entrance to the San Fernando hospital where he worked. At the impressive ceremony as told by the local newspaper, the tablet was covered in the Union Jack and was unveiled by the Honorary Surgeon General. It bears the following inscription and was erected by the Medical Society of Trinidad. It states as follows:
"In memory of Ernest Albert Turpin MB., Ch B. Edinburgh. Resident Surgeon of San Fernando Hospital 1910 -1922 Died at Port of Spain 18th March 1923. R.I.P."

I hope it is still there to this day. Ernest never married or had children. He died at the young age of 43. Mum used to talk about

# Chapter 3 Part 2 – Siblings of my Grandfather

"Uncle Ernest" with pride. She would have been only five when he died. It is clear when reading the newspaper describing Dr Ernest that he was a relative to be proud of. **See cutting and quotation from the newspaper article below.**

## THE UNVEILING.

Dr. Wise said he thought their hearts all of them, were full and very full with past remembrances and all he had to say was that that Memorial was unveiled to Dr. Turpin, a man whom they all honoured a man whom they all revered and a man whom they all loved.

## VOTE OF THANKS.

Dr. Vilain begged to move a hearty vote of thanks to the Hon. Surgeon General for having come down there

*"They saw his ability in his accurate diagnosis and treatment, and they also sadly realise their loss. As friend, as a member of the Society and as a brilliant Surgeon of the Colony. His place would take some time to fill.*
*His shortened life was in some measure due to the overworking of a not very robust constitution.*
*Dr Turpin was a strenuous, a staunch friend but of a retiring disposition. He devoted all his energy and time to the relief of others forgetful of his own health, another instance of a medical man dying at his post."*

**Cyril Anderson Turpin was born on 6th June 1880 probably in Barbados.**

Records appear to show that his place of birth was England. Simple logic would rule this out however as his mother Julia already had 2 small children, the youngest of whom would have been less than 18 months old. How would she have travelled to England to give birth to Cyril and leave two very young sons behind? Some mistake in the recording somewhere along the line, I fear. One theory is that he did have some medical treatment in London and may have claimed to be English in order to qualify for the treatment.

# From Barbados to Banffshire

Cyril travelled a lot and spent some twenty years big game hunting in Uganda as a game warden. He came back to live in Tobago and bought the cocoa plantation shares in Charlotteville from his father and Uncle Joseph.

**Photo taken at the Great House, Man o War Bay, Charlotteville**
Back Row - Stella, Milton, Gertrude, Rosalie (Totsie), Cyril
Front Row - Edmund (father), Sybil, Julia (mother), her Aunt Edith with her nurse. Charles Vivian is lying in front of his mother.
Photo taken circa 1900.

I have been sent a copy of a letter from Cyril to his sister Sybil (dated 28th August 1931 from Kampala, Uganda) where he seems to be lamenting the fact that he, as the most solvent member of the family, was expected to support others less financially secure. He married Ruby Smee in December 1934 quite late in his life and they had no children. Ruby died not long after they got married. My grandfather having had seven children, sometimes benefited from his brother's reluctant generosity. In the letter Cyril refers to how the "Milton fund" and other relatives appear to benefit from his wealth

# Chapter 3 Part 2 – Siblings of my Grandfather

more than he would prefer. "I always seem to be paying out and getting nothing back" he complains bitterly. "No sooner do I save 5/- than I am asked for 6/-" (shillings).

The following excerpt from Steve Sallfield's "A Brief History of Charlotteville Tobago" describes Cyril and his brother Charles involvement in Tobago:

*"Two of Edmond Turpin's sons, Charles V. Turpin the Crown Surveyor in Trinidad, and his brother Cyril A. Turpin a game warden in Uganda bought the shares of the Charlotteville and Pirate's Bay Estates and merged them into one in 1927. Plots of land from 5 to 50 acres had already been sold to some local families such as Murray, Nicholson, Carrington, and others, and the Turpin's' holdings were then around 1400 acres. (PT). Cyril Turpin was an avid naturalist and environmentalist and created a detailed management plan for the estate. Charles who was Crown Surveyor in Trinidad made a detailed survey of the estate. He planned the village on the lines of an English village with roads, a cricket pitch in the middle, and government offices. This formed the basis of the Charlotteville we know today. Patricia Turpin kindly gave me access to Cyril Turpin's exhaustive environmental plan which he sent from Kampala, Uganda, in 1932 and which aimed to make Charlotteville Estate and Pirates' Bay Estate into "one of the most beautiful places in the West Indies." From the economic point of view, he planned to establish a cocoa plantation of one million trees on 400 acres. He defined which areas would be for growing coconuts, limes, pigeon peas and coffee. To protect the environment, he planned a forest reserve where hunting and shooting would be forbidden. He outlined what was known about the spawning habits, feeding habits and life cycles of the indigenous kingfish, tuna, snappers and sharks and considered the tidal patterns and currents, so that local fishermen could work more effectively. Not all his ideas would have met with approval by today's environmentalists because he imported many foreign species of plants rather than focussing on the indigenous. He planned what he called an equatorial line passing through the estate, which was to be a double line of tropical trees, mostly ornamental like Jacaranda, Poinsettia, Red Flame of*

# From Barbados to Banffshire

*the Forest, Bougainvillea and Cassia. He sent seeds of plants from Ceylon, Malay states, Madagascar, and Australia as well as Uganda to Mr Malins-Smith the estate manager with strict instructions about which parts of the estate these were to be established in. (Documents of PT)"*

Despite all his travelling, and his heavy drinking Cyril lived longer than most of his siblings to reach the age of 77. He died on 16th March 1957 in Trinidad.

**Rosalie Agnes (Totsie) Turpin was born on 31st January 1882 in Barbados.**

Totsie was the affectionate pet name her family used for her. Although Mum would have been only 7 years old when her Aunt Totsie died, she did speak of her to us. She died in 1925 at the age of 43.

**Here is a photograph of Totsie acting in a school play with her brother Milton.** I don't believe either of them went on to pursue an acting career.

# Chapter 3 Part 2 – Siblings of my Grandfather

**My grandfather Milton Eyre Turpin was born on 14th August 1884 in Barbados.** (See Part 1 of this chapter)

**Edith Gertrude Turpin/Brisbane was born on 17th June 1886 in either Barbados or Tobago.**

Edith's father, Edmund Adolphus, is registered as having taken up a charge in St Andrews Church from 1886 – 1892 so she may have been born on either island. Mum referred to her as Aunt Gertie. She was married to Cecil Edward Brisbane.

This Aunt and Uncle played a very significant part in the lives of my mother and her sister Daphne. They stayed with them during the school holidays such as Christmas and Easter when they could not go home and boarded at the school during term time. This involved quite long periods when they were away from their parents in British Guiana. They could only go home for the long summer holidays as the boat journey from Trinidad to their home in Demerara was long and expensive. I'm not sure which part of the year was considered more of a "summertime" than any other time as unlike in Scotland, the temperature remains a steady 84 degrees F. throughout the year.

Mum spoke fondly of Aunt Gertie as well as her cousins, Joy, Dulcie, and Joan, to whom she seemed quite close. She described spending Christmas with her sister Daphne at her Aunt and Uncle's house as being a "different" experience to that enjoyed by her cousins. The cousins would put up a pillowcase each on Christmas Eve which would be filled with lovely presents. Mum and Daphne would only receive a couple of presents each. Mum was very philosophical about this and said she understood why it was different for them.

Dave and I met Dulcie and some of her family when we stayed with her at her home in Barbados in 1989. She was quite a character and used to get up early in the morning before 7am. She was a fit septuagenarian and would have had a good game of tennis before we were even awake. However, Dulcie did disappoint me with her

# From Barbados to Banffshire

racial prejudice as she would sit and complain when watching a mixed-race girl read the news on TV. She would shout at the screen, "Brown gal, Go home and mind baby," in her strong West Indian accent. "You people don't read the news." She would also grumble that she could not get "a boy" to work for her like before. This was in 1989!

Edith Gertrude Brisbane died of heart disease on 3rd January 1935 at the age of 49.

**Stella Lister Turpin was born on 30th September 1887 in Tobago**

Mum often spoke of Aunt Stella. She was glad of the support Stella gave her brother as he aged, as he suffered a lot of pain from arthritis. It is clear from his letters that he was very fond of Stella and relied on her quite a lot before and after his wife, Constance, died.

**Stella (see photo left)** married Charles Parkinson Stoute, a vet, on 9th February 1909 in St Vincent. They had five children. Charles Lister, Cyril Edmund, Ivor Parkinson, Sheila Mavis, and Keith Turpin. They lived mainly in Trinidad, but Stella made frequent trips to stay with her brother Milton in Guyana once the children were grown up.

Sheila Mavis married John Ince and they had two children Timothy Sheridan and Jeremy Martin. Timothy married Eileen Jones. Timothy and Eileen have done some of the genealogy work used for this book and they have sent me the family letters from which I have quoted.

Sheila was close to my mother growing up and they corresponded regularly when they were separated by the Atlantic. Sheila and John

# Chapter 3 Part 2 – Siblings of my Grandfather

very kindly accommodated Dave and I at their home in Trinidad when we visited in 1989 on our way to Tobago. Stella's personality as a caring person with a strong sense of family duty shines through in her letters. She died on 18th July 1954, in Port of Spain, Trinidad, just one year after my grandfather died. She was 64 years old.

**Charles Vivian Turpin was born on 27th January 1889 in Tobago.**

Charles became the Crown Surveyor for Trinidad and jointly owned Charlotteville Estate with his brother Cyril. He married an English girl, Mavis Sealey. Mavis had an identical twin sister called Iris. I met Iris a few times when she came to Scotland to visit my mother. **Mavis and Charles are pictured here in their wedding photograph.** I never met them but my mother and sister Gladys met with Mavis when they were in Tobago in 1979.

My mother used to describe Charles as a strict, rather puritanical man. He was not in favour of unmarried couples renting his cottages. If he discovered an unmarried couple occupying one of his cottages, he would insist they left immediately. He would knock on the door of the cottage regardless of the time of day or night and shout angrily at the couple telling them to leave immediately. Charles senior enjoyed quite robust health compared to his siblings. He outlived them all and died on 31st December 1975 at the age of 86.

Mavis and Charles had one son. Ernest Charles Sealy Turpin. He was born on 26th February 1937 in Tobago. We first met Charles and his second wife Patricia in 1989 at Charlotteville when we rented one of their cottages for a holiday. It was in an idyllic setting, a stone's throw from the beach and lovely warm sea. Mangoes were rolling about on the road, lovely juicy ones. I experienced my

# From Barbados to Banffshire

one and only attempt at snorkelling not far from the cottages and enjoyed it very much.

 **Charles pictured left** loved to sing and play the guitar, calypso style. He had a rich baritone, very musical voice. He often entertained the holiday makers who came to the Man O' War Bay cottages to soak up the sun, and swim and snorkel in the area. Charles seemed to be the complete opposite in character to what my mother described his father to be. He was a great storyteller too and kept us spellbound with his stories of hunting for buried treasure on the beach and surrounding countryside.

We visited the Man O' War Bay cottages once in 1989 and then again in 1993. As you enter the front of the present Great House it is impossible to miss the heads of the various wild animals which reflect Uncle Cyril's African game hunting past. The house is very atmospheric. Mavis Turpin, wife of Charles Vivian, used to say the house was haunted. My mother and sister Gladys, her husband Peter and their two smallest children at that time, Milton and Leanne, visited in 1979. Gladys was convinced she did experience some spooky goings on in the night. She told me she heard people chatting in their holiday cottage when she knew the others were asleep.

When Dave and I visited, the voices did not chat in our cottage, but I did feel the sense of history and some intrigue when visiting the Great House. The roof of the Great House is mainly covered by corrugated iron supported by substantial wooden beams. We were told that a snake could sometimes be seen patrolling the exposed rafters above, looking for vermin. When walking on the beach near our holiday cottage we observed one of these huge snakes constricting and devouring a large rat. We could see the form of the unfortunate rat proceeding through the snake's body. Quite a sight to behold. Unfortunately, the snake itself was then cruelly beaten to death with sticks by local youths. We were told the locals believe the snakes contain evil spirits.

**The Great House Charlotteville Tobago 1989**

Tobago had a colourful, rather blood thirsty history of piracy as well as slavery. The island was fought over by the French, the Dutch, the Spanish and the British constantly during the 17th - 19th centuries. It changed hands 33 times. Tobago was eventually colonised along with Trinidad in 1889 by the British Empire. It remained under British rule until, along with Trinidad became a Commonwealth country in 1962. It did not become a full republic until 1976.

When Charles visited us here in Scotland later that same year, we made some recordings of him singing at a party we had at our home for him. We had a great night of music and song. We still have the recordings.

# From Barbados to Banffshire

Charles was first married to Diane. They had 2 children Joanne and Charles. Their marriage ended in divorce after Diane had accompanied her children to England for their education. She told me that she had not liked the climate in Tobago. I became acquainted with their family through my Ancestry.com membership when Joanne's daughter Caitlin was identified as a DNA match. When Dave and I visited Barbados in 2019 we rented a flat in Diane's holiday villa in Holetown for two weeks. Diane has recently retired and is living in England to be nearer her family.

Charles' second marriage was to Patricia, a local girl. They had two children Ryan and Christine. Patricia still lives in the Great House in Tobago and has become an authority on environmental issues in the island. She has made a study of the plant life and wildlife and has represented Tobago at environmental conferences in Paris. Ryan has two daughters, Mahala and Catherine and Christine has one son called Nathan. They live in Florida.

Charles died on 17th September 2002.

**Sybil Alice Turpin was born on 1st October 1890, probably in Tobago.**

Sybil was the youngest of Edmund and Julia's children. I know very little about her other than that she did not enjoy good health. She married James Punnet and they had three children, Ken, Valarie and Ernest. Sybil died in 1945 at the age of 55.

# Chapter 4 Part 1 – My Mother's Story

**Constance Margot Turpin Weir was born on 13th October 1918 in Barbados**.

My mother was the third daughter of Canon Milton Eyre Turpin and Constance Margaret Clark Gray Turpin.

I am beginning her story with her account of her life in her own words taken from a book called "A Life Recalled for My Grandchild." Her answers are prompted by questions in the book. I asked her to complete the questions in 1996 for my daughter Pamela on her marriage to her first husband Kenny on 22nd June 1996.

These are her answers in her own words copied from the book:

*"I was born at 7pm on Sunday Evening and my father was unable to take the service that evening. My family lived in Barbados, then Fort Wellington, British Guiana.*

*My brothers and sisters were Grace Julia Mary, Gertrude Daphne (both older than me), James Edmund Michael, Christine Eyre, Milton Everett Andrew, and Guy Oswald Garnet.*

*My Early Childhood*

*My favourite toys were dolls, crayons, paints, making dolls clothes on my mother's sewing machine.*

*My favourite stories were Grimms Fairy Tales, and Aesop's Fables, and Bible Stories.*

*I liked playing hopscotch, snap, skipping, hide and seek, and party games, with my dolls.*

*I started school when I was six years old. My childhood quirks were dressing up, singing, and dancing the Charleston. I taught my sister Christine to dance.*

*Things I remember about my parents: .... Every Easter Monday my father took us all on a kite flying picnic, he also played cricket and other games with us all. My mother played the piano and sang lovely songs and was full of fun, played skipping games with us all,*

# From Barbados to Banffshire

*and taught us dances that she did when a young girl, also all the Nursery Rhymes.*

*My School Days*

*My first school was a private school in Port of Spain, Trinidad.*

*My school uniform was navy skirt, white blouse, red and black tie.*

*My best lessons were Botany, History, French, Needlework.*

*At playtime we played cricket and rounders and netball.*

*Things I remember about my first school. There were only 20 pupils, more girls than boys. My teacher's name was Miss Moore and we were taught at her house. I lived with my Aunt Gertrude in Port of Spain, Trinidad but went home to Guyana for the long school holidays.*

*My secondary school was The Bishops High School, Port of Spain, Trinidad.*

*The uniform was navy pleated skirts with white blouses, black and red ties and a Panama hat with a red and black band.*

*My favourite subjects were Arithmetic, Needlework, French, Divinity, Art, Botany, English, History and Latin.*

*Teachers could punish us by order marks. 1 for a small offence, 2 for a bad offence. When you got 10 your name went into a black book.*

*Prizes were awarded for Needlework and all subjects.*

*Sports I played at school were cricket, rounders, and netball.*

*Clubs I belonged to were Girl Guides and Gymnasium.*

*Special positions I held were Tawny Owl. I was too young to be Brown Owl.*

*My Teenage Years.*

*When I was a teenager, my family lived in British Guiana, but I lived in Port of Spain, Trinidad where I was at Boarding School.*

# Chapter 4 Part 1 – My Mother's Story

*My ambitions were to be a ballet dancer, and acting, singing and dancing. In my spare time I read books, taught myself to sew, make frocks for my dolls and was able to make party frocks for my sister Christine, yes, I still played with dolls at the age of thirteen.*

*At weekends, I went to church on Sundays, visited my relations and friends, went on seaside picnics staying in the sea all day long; well off and on.*

*I liked to spend money on materials for dressmaking and crepe paper for paper roses, also coloured pencils and paint books. My money came from pocket money and birthday gifts etc.*

*While at school in Trinidad I was taken with fellow boarders to listen to Ignace Jan Paderewski, Polish Concert Pianist who was touring the West Indies in 1934.*

*The fashion rage was frocks with tiny waists, and full skirts, maxi length, wavy curly hair style, any length, sandals, court shoes and silk stockings. What I remember about boyfriends were my brother Michael's friends and friends of the family and those I met at teenage parties. They all had such lovely manners.*

*Things which used to make me happy were family concerts and outings with my parents and doing well at school and going to parties where there would be dancing.*

*I also taught the local Girl Guides Country Dancing.*

*Things that used to upset me were Thunder and Lightning and illness in the family i.e., Malaria.*

*When I left school, I went home to British Guiana and had a private school at the Rectory, also a Brownie Pack in my sole charge. I later became a governess to a little four-year-old girl, Eve Mowat, who lived on a sugar estate called Cane grove, her father was the manager of the estates."*

Mum then goes on to describe how she met my father at a party on Dekinderen Estate where he worked in 1935. She was 17 years old, and he was 34. She liked him because, "*I felt secure in his company*". He told her he liked her because "*I was different*". She

# From Barbados to Banffshire

told me that she also liked that he had several suits as most of the other men she met did not wear suits. They enjoyed horse-riding together, playing tennis and attending dinner dances as well as going to the cinema.

My mother describes a beautiful wedding which took place on 29th April 1940. They were married by Allan John Knight, Bishop of Guiana in St Simon's Church, Dekinderen, Demerara, British Guiana.

*"The Bishop's mother carried a basket of pink rose petals which she threw over us as we left the church. There were 60 - 70 guests at the wedding reception which was held at the Dekinderen Manager's House. There were speeches with champagne and a dance afterward."*

Their first night as a married couple was spent in the Tower Hotel, Georgetown, followed by a week, honeymooning in Bartica. I must say it would not have been my first choice for a honeymoon destination (see "Guyana Holiday 1993" at the end of Chapter 4.2).

A bungalow had been built especially for the newly married couple but when Dad became Manager of the Dekinderen sugar plantation they moved into the Manager's house. My sisters Margaret, Gladys, and I were all born in Corunna Nursing Home, Georgetown, while the family were living in Dekinderen House. Apart from Dad's intermittent bouts of ill health, we all enjoyed a seemingly idyllic existence in Demerara. We were in close contact with Mum's parents Grandpa and Granny Turpin, who did not live far away.

# Chapter 4 Part 1 – My Mother's Story

**Below is a photograph of Dekinderen Estate House where we lived.**

## Leaving Demerara

When my parents had been married only 7 years, their whole world was set to change quite dramatically, especially for my mother. My father had been unable to visit his home country of Scotland for his leave entitlement due to the war which had been raging in Europe during that period. Dad made arrangements to take his whole family to Scotland to meet his mother and sisters for the first time as well as for him to have an essential health check in his home country.

Although word had reached my parents that Britain was experiencing one of the worst winters in living memory, they had to go ahead with their plans.

My mother said her goodbyes to her family and friends, fully expecting to be returning to her home in Demerara after a few months' holiday. She was blissfully unaware that her life would take such a dramatic turn and she would never see her mother again.

# From Barbados to Banffshire

She was leaving her friends, her horses, and colonial lifestyle, which she had been used to all her life, for ever. She was 28 years old.

On the 3rd of March 1947 we boarded a troop ship from Georgetown, calling in past Tobago and the Virgin Islands for England. The name of the ship was the "Strategist". We stopped in Tobago for Mum to say goodbye to her Uncle Charles and Aunt Mavis at Man O' War Bay, Charlotteville.

The journey must have been quite an ordeal, especially since my mother was four months pregnant with my sister Betty. We disembarked 16 days later on the 19th of March and went to stay in Rickmansworth, near London, with my father's sister Peg, her husband, Dr Hilton Willcox, and their three children, Hylton, Ian, and Margaret, for about a week. My cousin Ian, aged 7 at the time, recalls that they had snow and that my sisters and I were excited to see snow for the first time. We then made the journey to Banff to stay with my grandmother at her home called "Helenslea" in Seafield Street, Banff.

**Arrival in Banff**

While Grandma Weir did try to make my mother feel welcome, the complete change of climate and culture was very difficult for my mother to adjust to. Mum had never learned to cook, having always had servants. She often talked fondly of the lady she called "Cook". She also used to say without any hint of embarrassment that, "*She was as black as the Ace of Spades.*" Mum would have been horrified if someone told her that she was making a racist comment.

Grandma took on the task of teaching Mum to cook. Some of Grandma's cooking methods were quite a shock for Mum, such as when she saw her boil eggs in the kettle used for boiling the water for making the tea. Mum had had to be extra careful with hygiene coming from such a hot country.

Mum told me of how she experienced a somewhat frosty atmosphere from her sisters in law at first. She had been told they

# Chapter 4 Part 1 – My Mother's Story

were quite critical of my father for marrying someone so much younger than himself. My father's two younger sisters, Nell and Frances had trained to become hoteliers, and worked in the Crown Hotel in Banff, which their father had bought when he retired from farming (see the next chapter - My Father's Story). Mum understood the real reason for the frosty reception when she later learned from my father's solicitor that, prior to her arrival in Scotland, "a friend" who had arrived back in Scotland from Demerara had warned my aunts that my mother, being the wife of the oldest son, would expect to take over the hotel or at least have a share in it. The solicitor had been told of this by my father's sisters and had been asked by them to draw up a legal document in order to ensure this could not happen. "*Nothing could have been farther from the truth*", Mum said.

I can't imagine how lost and alone she must have felt. She was a very uncomplaining sort of person and just kept her feelings to herself. The first people Mum met to whom she felt able to relate were Agnes and George Campbell. They lived in Fraserburgh with their daughter Jean aged 5 at that time, and also with Agnes's sister Bess. The sisters were my father's first cousins. They seemed more understanding of Mum's plight than Dad's sisters were. We used to visit each other quite often. They welcomed us all into their family in a genuine friendly manner.

## Moving House

After living in Banff for about 6 months, our family moved to a house called Rose Cottage in Cuminestown, a village approximately 14 miles from Banff. We lived there until 1949 when my father bought Crossroads Farm, Rothiemay, with the help of a loan from his mother. "*Paid back in full*", Mum made sure to tell anyone who wanted to know.

This move brought even more stress for my mother, who had at least had the luxury of electricity in Grandma's house as well as the cottage in Cuminestown. Tilly lamps were the main source of lighting. Sometimes, when they caught fire, Mum would let out a bloodcurdling shriek as the flames almost reached the ceiling.

# From Barbados to Banffshire

Fortunately, Dad was near at hand and was able to deal with these incidents appropriately.

## Life on the Farm

The occupants of the farm cottage belonging to the farm would help Mum with looking after the younger children and did other general housework. Dad employed several farm hands for whom Mum had to cook. They enjoyed her cooking as they told her she gave them better meals than the other farmer's wives. However, on one occasion I remember my father having a squad of men at the farm to operate a "steam mill" to thrash the corn. Mum had about 12 men to give lunch to. On one occasion she made rice pudding but accidentally put in salt instead of sugar. Most of the men quietly ate the pudding without a word until one man called Ned said, "*Missus you've put salt in the pudding*". Mum was very apologetic and so ashamed of her mistake.

There was a bedroom, known as the "chammer" (chamber) above the coal shed in which the full-time farm hand would live. It was extremely basic with no "mod cons". On one occasion I remember visiting the resident farmworker called Tom, while he was the occupant of the "chammer". He told me he was visited by rats during the night. He said he would be awakened by the rats chewing his ears. I was aghast and spellbound at the same time, listening to "Old Tom" as we called him describing his night-time visitors. After Tom left, we had Bert living in the "chammer" and he stayed with us until the farm was sold in 1966. Mum was not happy about us visiting the men in their accommodation and said it was strictly against the rules.

Mum used to get up very early in the mornings and light the Raeburn cooker, so that the kitchen was above freezing when we got up for breakfast, before going to school. When I managed to convince Mum that I was ill enough to stay off school, I loved listening to a morning radio programme called "Music While You Work" as well as "having my mother all to myself". Sometimes she would put on a coat and scarf, which made me ask where she was going. Her reply was, "I'm going upstairs to make the beds."

# Chapter 4 Part 1 – My Mother's Story

Only a few months after we moved into the farm, in 1949, Mum received the incredibly sad news that her beloved mother Constance, who we referred to as Grannie Turpin, had died. She was terribly upset. Mum had always tried to protect us from any deep sadness in the family as she used to cope with sorrow best by denying it to herself. The tragic news coming so soon after Mum had crossed the Atlantic in the opposite direction from which her mother had travelled, away from her family in Edinburgh, does seem like history repeating itself. It must have been one of the hardest things Mum had to cope with after leaving British Guiana in 1947.

During her life on the farm Mum did her best to be a good "farmer's wife". She joined the local WRI (Women's Rural Institute) and became more well known in the community. She was President of the Women's Guild at one time and even became proficient at public speaking. My sister Gladys recalls the occasion when Mum was asked to present the prizes at Rothiemay Primary school. She was delighted to be asked to do this. I had left Rothiemay School by this time.

Mum loved sewing and would spend any spare time she had making clothes for our dolls as well as ourselves. She would sit up half the night to get something finished. It was lovely to wake up in the morning and find the result of her labours at the foot of our beds. Our dolls did not realise how lucky they were.

There was a large family who lived in the village one mile from our house. Their mother's name was Bessie. She was a single parent and she struggled to make ends meet. Mum felt sorry for her and befriended Bessie. One day I remember arriving home from school to find Bessie and her children in the garden. We had heard children at the school calling them names and we were shocked to find them there. We rather unkindly questioned Mum as to why she had invited them to OUR house. I'm so ashamed of this uncaring attitude. I don't think Dad was happy about this friendship either. He did not share my mother's altruism. She only came the once.

# From Barbados to Banffshire

## Stories of Life in British Guiana

We children loved to hear our mother reminisce about her life in the tropics. She would fondly refer to the Vicarage where she lived with her parents and siblings during their childhood as "The Wreckerage". The incredibly old rundown building had holes in the floor which the children had to jump across, and sometimes they fell through the rotten floorboards. She was not complaining but told the story as if it was a huge joke. I can still hear her laugh about it.

The family was not well off. Mum was aware of her father's meagre remuneration as an Anglican priest so did not expect to be given expensive presents at birthdays or Christmas. Mum said they did not suffer hardship as the wealthy parishioners often donated their no longer needed expensive clothes and toys to "the parson's children". They were invited to all the best parties and mixed with the "higher echelons of colonial society" despite their relatively impoverished circumstances. A wealthy dentist, Mr Doobay, who was a close family friend, arranged for my mother and sister Daphne to be educated at the exclusive boarding school in Trinidad, known as "The Bishop's High School".

An interesting coincidence happened about ten years ago when my friends, Penny and Bob Selbie, found themselves sharing a table with Patamba Doobay's daughter Leila Doobay and her husband while on holiday in Italy. When Leila mentioned she came from Guyana, my friends immediately mentioned their friendship with me. Leila could hardly believe the coincidence and told them how close our families had been. I wrote to her, and she replied, confirming that their family were fond of us as well as my grandparents. She also mentioned my nanny Lilian who she said was an Indian girl, confirming my memory of Lilian. Her father was indeed the Indian dentist and doctor, Patamba Doobay, and he had looked after all our health needs. Leila had been 14 years old when she knew us.

One of our favourite stories, which Mum told of her life as a young mother in Dekinderen plantation house, was about the pet parrot called Robert. The parrot could speak and if my mother was calling the cook to discuss what was for dinner, the parrot would shriek

# Chapter 4 Part 1 – My Mother's Story

"Cook! Cook!" echoing my mother's voice. The parrot could spell its name too and could be heard chanting "R.O.B.E.R.T. Robert". I'm not sure who was given the credit for training the parrot, but we loved to hear this story repeated over and over again. There was also a pet monkey which used to pick insects from my hair and eat them. My hair was very sparse and white as a child, so the monkey could spy the insects easily. I have no recollection of this experience.

When it was raining heavily on the farm, and Mum was feeling homesick, she would go out and sit in the coal shed listening to the rain battering the corrugated iron roof. She found it comforting.

## The Farmer's Wife

I often feel we did not let our mother know just how good a mother she was to us all. Mum was under no illusion that she was "a good farmer's wife". My aunts and grandmother may have inadvertently contributed to her feelings of inadequacy as they would make a point of telling her that a good farmer's wife always had tins of home baking ready to produce when unexpected visitors arrived. Visitors would turn up without warning in farming communities. Mum did try to be that farmer's wife and baked whenever she had time. She would live in dread of unexpected visitors arriving when she had nothing in the tins.

One of my happiest memories while growing up on the farm was when on a Saturday night Mum would read us weekly instalments of the novel "Little Women" by Louisa M. Alcott. This was the story of a family of four girls, Meg, Jo, Beth and Amy and their parents. We each identified with one of them. The oldest was called Meg so she was my sister Margaret, I was Jo, the outspoken one, Gladys was Amy, the pretty one, and Betty was Beth who did not have good health (Betty had diabetes). Avril was still too young to worry that there was no one for her to be identified with. In the story, one Christmas, the mother took their Christmas dinner to a poor family down the road and the girls got bread and cheese. I lived in dread our mother would do the same one day. How selfish is that!

# From Barbados to Banffshire

Mum also made sure we had a good Christmas with presents such as board games and skipping ropes. Dad used to complain that he should not have to hand over "a whole ten pounds" for her to buy us presents; but I can remember her insisting. She rarely challenged him about anything else. We felt lucky because our school friends told us they received nothing at Christmas, but they got "an orange and an apple" at Hogmanay. My "big" present was a "Girls Crystal" annual.

### Mum and Dad dancing at a Farmers' Ball in Huntly in the 1950's

Mum and Dad were able to enjoy their love of ballroom dancing occasionally when they attended farmers' balls.

My parents lived on the farm with my younger sisters, Gladys, Betty, and Avril after Margaret, and I had left home for work or marriage. When the farm was sold in 1966, they moved to the town of Banff.

During their married life Dad had intermittent bouts of ill health which deteriorated as he aged. Mum cared for him and catered for his increasing needs very competently and selflessly. Dad often spoke of his appreciation for the way she cared for him night and day.

### Widowhood in Ellon

After Dad died in March 1971, Mum moved to the small town of Ellon to be closer to the farm where my sister Gladys lives with her husband Peter and family. Mum seemed to settle into her widowhood with the same degree of acceptance of change which she had displayed throughout her life. She joined the local Anglican Church of St Mary on the Rock and became a regular attender. Mum joined the local Bridge club and enjoyed this hobby at which she excelled. She was not available for babysitting any Monday night as Bridge night was not to be missed for any reason. She also became involved in collecting for charities such as Christian Aid, Cancer Research, and the Red Cross.

My mother's most favourite hobby of all was ballroom dancing which she had enjoyed with my father in his younger days, before his poor health stopped that. An old friend of my parents when they lived in British Guiana, Roy Skinner, became her most regular dancing partner. He was almost a member of the family and was often present at family parties. At these parties he liked to recite quite long poems in Scots dialect by poets such as J. C. Milne. This caused a lot of nervous hilarity as the grandchildren fought hard to stifle their giggles. Roy made no attempt to hide his disapproval at their lack of appreciation of his literary prowess. He used to test their mental arithmetic at the dinner table, even at Christmas time. He thought the standard of education on offer was appalling when they struggled to provide the answer to three figured multiplication sums.

Roy was of similar age to my father but had enjoyed better health. He used to take Mum on trips to other parts of Scotland where there were dinner dances being held and she enjoyed these trips immensely. Separate rooms were essential, however, as Mum made it clear to anyone who asked why, declaring "*I've had enough of that nonsense.*" They became quite well known in the neighbourhood as excellent dancers. Mum used to say she felt like a teenager on the dance floor.

My mother was one of those people who could light up a room and was usually the "life and soul" of any party or gathering at which she was present. She would always be the self-appointed mistress of ceremonies. I can still hear her voice announcing, "*Pamela will now play the violin*", followed by Roy's voice loudly demanding "*The Flooer O' the Quern.*" It was his favourite tune. Pamela did not dare to disappoint. We were all summoned in turn to do our party piece. Mum would sing her songs she learned as a child such as "Navaho"

# From Barbados to Banffshire

and "I Don't Want to Play in Your Yard". Video recordings of these songs are available on YouTube.

Mum disapproved of any disagreements within the family. When my son David was experiencing a manic episode, I would be concerned that he would turn up at her door presenting bizarre behaviour. He did visit her on some of these occasions but seemed to manage to behave normally when he was in her presence. At times when I tracked him down by phone to her house, she would tell me confidently. "*There is nothing wrong with David. We are having a cup of tea.*" David would have been first in the queue to sing her praises as he often did in his poetry. They had a very close relationship and although he knew her quality of life for her last years was extremely poor, he was devastated when she died in 2008... Here is a poem David wrote for one of her birthdays:

## Grandma

*There's no one quite like Margot, She's really most unique*
*And when it comes to dance and fashion, She's always tres tres chic*

*I really like the way she walks, With no glimmer of a waddle*
*But the reason is so plain to see, She's the model for a model*

*When you've had an awful year, and your world is left in rubble*
*Grandma lifts you up again, Sends you plaudits for your trouble*

*Young people meeting Grandmama, who think she is the Queen*
*Get really disappointed when they see the real 'een*

*So Happy Birthday Grandma, we love you one and all*
*That's enough of this old poem, Let's make this gig a ball!*

# Chapter 4 Part 1 – My Mother's Story

## 2004 – 2008

These last four years of my mother's life were the saddest in the lives of all her close family. When we all gathered to celebrate her 86th birthday at a restaurant on 13th October 2004, we had no idea that this was to be the last time she was able to hold a meaningful conversation with us. Mum suffered a major stroke and collapsed at her home two days later when she had been expecting a visit from her granddaughter Pamela, husband Kenny and their two small children Owen and Roisin. They arrived to find her collapsed on the hall floor of her bungalow. She had to be rushed to Aberdeen Royal Infirmary that day.

After an initial assessment in that hospital, she spent a number of months in Woodend Hospital in Aberdeen before being moved to Maud Hospital in East Aberdeenshire for a further few months. Her personality had changed, and the light had gone out of her eyes. Conversation was almost impossible. She could only repeat what was said to her rather than take part in a conversation. She was eventually moved to Auchtercrag Nursing Home in Ellon. We all took it in turns to visit her almost daily, but she did not improve. We could not get her back to her old self.

A few months later after taking up residence in the Nursing Home, in 2006, she had another stroke, resulting in the loss of her ability to swallow food. She had to have a feeding tube inserted. Mum could still hear and enjoy music which she had listened to in the past and she could still see us, recognise us and watch the snooker on television. However, in January 2008 a further even more devastating stroke caused her to be completely bedridden and blind. We continued to take turns to visit her daily but there was no improvement. When she died on 10th July 2008, we felt it must have been a welcome relief for her as well as us, her closest family. Nevertheless, it was still a tragic loss which left a huge hole in our lives. Life was so unfair for someone who was a truly kind and caring person herself.

My mother's funeral was conducted in St Mary on the Rock Church, Ellon by her good friend the Very Reverend Gerald Stranraer Mull.

# From Barbados to Banffshire

She is buried in Banff Cemetery beside my father and his family. Thus, her journey ended, and she is the true heroine of this book entitled "From Barbados to Banffshire". Her journey had indeed started with her birth in Barbados, then moving to British Guiana at the age, of three. She lived there for 25 years before moving to Banffshire which is now an integrated part of Aberdeenshire in Scotland.

The year 2008 was one of the saddest years I have ever experienced in my life, in fact in the history of our whole family. In March we lost Paul (27), son of Gladys and Peter. This was a dreadfully shocking tragedy, which traumatised us all. Mum died on 10th July, not a shock, but an incredibly sad end to such a kind caring beautiful soul. The family then suffered another shock when my son David (43), took his own life in the November. (More about this in my own story). Then in December of that same year, my husband Dave suffered a heart attack from which I'm glad to say he has made a full recovery.

In part two of this chapter, I describe Mum's sisters and brothers who have all had interesting lives worthy of a book of their own.

**From left to right:**
**Christine, Michael, Margot (Mum), Daphne and Grace**

# Chapter 4 Part 2 – Maternal Aunts and Uncles

## Grace Julia Mary Turpin was born on 1st October 1915

Aunt Grace was born in Bartica, British Guiana when her father was working there as an Anglican priest.

Medical facilities were primitive, and my mother told us that Grace's birth was very difficult. She was a large baby, and my grandmother was a small woman, less than 5 feet tall. The house they lived in was remote and although a doctor was called to attend to the birth, he took a long time to get there. When he did arrive, the birth was imminent. The doctor had come from a dinner party and seemed intoxicated, according to what my grandfather told my mother. The baby was coming in the breech position and the doctor said his priority was to save the mother. The baby became brain damaged during the birth and suffered spine damage. My mother said that the doctor did not make much attempt to treat the baby. After he left, Grace did show signs of life and her parents were able to revive her and care for her with only minimal medical help. Grandpa Turpin's work in the Bartica Mission ended in 1916 and their daughters Daphne, Margot and son Michael were born in Barbados, where the medical facilities were better.

Grace inevitably suffered from developmental delay and did not walk unaided until she was 5 years old. She was also slow to talk, and her parents were told that she was unlikely to be able to learn to read and write so she did not attend school.

Grace was dearly loved and well looked after by her parents. She lived quite happily with her family during her childhood. Unfortunately, when she reached a delayed puberty in her late teens, she began to display disturbing behaviour such as screaming loudly out of the windows and banging doors in frustration. Doctors in Guyana did not have the skills to help Grace or advise her parents on how to care for her. They told them that the only option was an asylum in the capital, Georgetown. This would have been very traumatic for Grace and her family. The Bishop of Guyana became involved, and he advised that she be taken to England to

# From Barbados to Banffshire

live with her Aunt Chris in order to have access to specialist help there.

Her parents were devastated to have to part with Grace and send her all the way across the Atlantic Ocean. Her baby brother Guy Oswald was less than one year old so Grace could not be accompanied by her mother. She was accompanied on the voyage by a nursing sister called Rosaleen Veecock and a Clerk of Holy Orders called William F. Reeves (information from Ancestry.com). She did not know these people. Grace boarded a ship called the "Ingria" and left Demerara in August 1933. She arrived in London via Grenada and Barbados on 3rd September 1933. Grace was then met by her Aunt Chris and her son-in-law Claude Forsyth. who took her to their home in Runcorn Cheshire.

One year later when Granny Turpin travelled to England hoping to take Grace back with her, she was advised that Grace should remain in England. At one point they were asked to give permission for a lobotomy to be performed, but my grandfather refused to sign the papers. My grandmother was heartbroken to have to return home without Grace.

My information is unclear as to what Grace's movements were from then on. I know she spent some time in Larbert Mental Hospital in Scotland, and subsequently was moved between various nursing homes. Growing up we were only vaguely aware that we had a disabled aunt living in the UK. When we asked about her, my mother became upset, so we learned not to bring up the subject until we were adults.

After my father died in 1971 Gladys and Peter took Mum to visit Grace from time to time and she was pleased to see them. After I met Dave, who belonged to Edinburgh, we made a point of visiting Grace in her nursing home in Strathyre on our way home from visits to his parents in Edinburgh.

My mother and Grace loved singing the songs their mother taught them. We recorded Mum singing these songs on a tape and sent it

# Chapter 4 Part 2 – Maternal Aunts and Uncles

to Grace. She enjoyed listening and singing along with the tapes in the Nursing Home. Granny Turpin and Grace had the same clear soft skin, quite wrinkle free. My mother often remarked on it when we visited Grace in the nursing home.

We considered moving Grace nearer to where we lived in Aberdeenshire but were always told she was very settled in the home she lived in. This changed however, when the Social Work Department phoned us one morning and said they were seriously concerned with the standard of care being provided by the care managers in Grace's nursing home. They told us that the home was being investigated and was likely to be closed. We then arranged to bring Grace up to Aberdeenshire in 1993 where she was placed in a Nursing Home near Ellon.

We had not had concerns about the previous place or her care because she seemed quite happy, and the Care Home Manager seemed to be fond of Grace. It did not seem to matter where Grace was placed, she always seemed to be content with her lot and oblivious to any difficulties. We were assured that Grace had not been subjected to any physical abuse, but we later learned that her savings had been misappropriated.

There were times when my mother and I would look through Grace's wardrobe or closet as she called it for clothes which did not fit. We did this in order to make room for the new ones we brought, as requested by the Care Home Manager. "*Don't rake!*" she would shout. I found this very understandable. It was an indication to us of how institutionalised she had become with no sense of control of her own life.

We were able to visit Aunt Grace regularly and get to know her once she was living in Aberdeenshire. Sadly, by this time she was 78 years old. She would also tell us on more than one occasion that she was born in Bartica and say, "*I was put in a box and left for dead.*" I am not sure whom she had overheard saying this, but my mother said it was not strictly true. This indicated to me that she had

# From Barbados to Banffshire

more understanding than she had been given credit for and had overheard people talking about her as if she wasn't there.

Grace often talked about her parents as if they were still alive and about to visit her at any time. It didn't matter how often we told her they had died, she preferred to live in her dream world where they were still alive. When we visited, she would talk very fondly of her childhood and could remember details about the presents she received at Christmas. She was particularly fond of a manicure set which she said her sister Daphne had tried to say was hers. They had had a fight about it. She would give us a "blow by blow" account of the fight. She mentioned Daphne a lot, probably as she was the oldest sister after herself. Daphne felt responsible for Grace throughout her life and made sure that she received birthday and Christmas presents every year. She would send money to my mother for her to buy presents for Grace, wherever she was living.

Grace had a sunny disposition which helped her to cope with her situation and, we hope, afforded her better care as she was so well liked by all her carers in the many different settings in which she found herself. Reports from the various caregivers always said things like; "Grace is no trouble and seems very contented with her lot." and "She is such a happy soul and a joy to look after."

# Chapter 4 Part 2 – Maternal Aunts and Uncles

The following poem was written by my son David, for his Great Aunt Grace on her 90th birthday. He also read it out at her funeral in 2006.

*Grace, Grace your smiling face*
*Is like a shining moon through lace*
*Your voice is like a summer wind*
*When you sing your childhood songs*
*I don't know when they'll make the charts*
*But I'm sure it won't be long*
*Grace, Grace you've found a place*
*In all our hearts and lives*
*And your friendship means so much to us*
*That some of us don't need wives*
*You have a special view of things*
*That can often be a startle*
*But why oh why must you leave your gifts*
*Still wrapped up in their parcels???*

Aunt Grace died on 23rd October 2006 at the age of 91. David and Grace share their final resting place in Ellon Cemetery. Grace had the longest life of all her siblings and was the only member of the family to live beyond her 90th birthday.

## Gertrude Daphne Turpin was born on 17th June 1917

Gertrude Daphne (known as Daphne) born in Barbados, was the second daughter born to my maternal grandparents and had to embrace the role of oldest daughter due to her older sister Grace's disability. I think Daphne must have had to develop independence early in her life as Grace required most of her parents' attention. Daphne developed a very resilient nature and strength of character.

# From Barbados to Banffshire

My mother and Daphne had to travel to Boarding School in Trinidad to receive their education as British Guiana did not have a particularly good standard of education to offer them. Daphne was a good scholar with a strong personality and Mum looked to her for leadership throughout their childhood. We grew up very aware of the significance of Daphne as my mother's big sister.

Daphne was a beautiful woman and had many suitors. She was quite flamboyant and very much her own woman, knowing what she wanted out of life and how to get it.... well almost. Her marriage was not altogether a happy one but that is not my story to tell.

Daphne married Roy Asdaile Simpson, an English colonel in the British Army, after a whirlwind romance of about a week. This ended her engagement to another young man called Jackie. Mum told us that he was "*a very sweet young man*", and that he was heartbroken. He had been well liked by the family, and they were disappointed that Daphne did not give them the opportunity to get to know Roy before they married.

Roy and Daphne left her parents' home quite suddenly and travelled over to England in July 1938. They were married in Willesden, Middlesex where Roy's parents lived, within a few days of their arrival in England. They returned home soon after that but left for Barranquilla, Columbia a year later where their first child Clive Edward Asdaile Simpson was born on 18th April 1940. They returned to British Guiana before Roy was called to join the war in Europe.

My mother recalled a family dinner where Roy announced that he was leaving British Guiana to join in the war effort in England. Daphne wanted to go with him, and she asked my grandparents to look after Clive for them while they were away. Grandpa was very angry about this, and Mum told us she remembered him thumping the table with anger shouting "*No, No, No*", very upset that Daphne was prepared to leave such a young child so that she could join Roy and take part in the war. He was particularly angry that she was prepared to risk losing her life in Europe. Daphne was very persuasive, however, and her parents agreed to look after Clive who was only one year old at the time.

Mum described Clive as an adorable little boy, with golden curls, who became closely attached to his grandparents. She told of how his parents arrived back at the end of the war in 1945 with their beautiful baby girl Lois Anne, who had been born in Edinburgh in May 1944. Lois told me that her mother decided to give birth to her in Edinburgh because German bombs were bombarding London. Another reason was that a close family friend, Sir James Learmonth (an eminent surgeon who had attended the royal family), practised in Edinburgh and was willing to deliver the baby.

Clive was almost 5 years old when they returned and was very shy of his parents. He preferred his grandmother to Daphne for whom he had no memory. Mum said that when Daphne tried to pick him up, he ran away from her to his Granny saying, "*I don't want to go to any old mother*". It's funny how these stories stick in your mind. I don't believe their relationship ever recovered from the separation.

Daphne did enjoy her time in England. She worked in an administrative role at Bletchley Park (famous for the Enigma project). She was also required to function as a driver for Army personnel. She was a member of the First Aid Nursing Yeomanry F.A.N.Y. known affectionately as Fannies. Roy saw action in Europe and was quite a war hero.

After the war they returned to live in Barranquilla, Columbia where their youngest son Alec Nevile was born in 1946.

# From Barbados to Banffshire

Daphne's only daughter Lois takes up the story here:

"*Mummy had a very active life in Baranquilla. When she was pregnant with Clive, Daddy was shot near the heart by a robber at the Frontino Gold mines which was either on or near our finca Yerba Buena. Mum tried to get a German pilot to fly him to the nearest hospital, but he refused as our countries were on the brink of war. Mum rode to the nearest hospital on horseback & finally got him help. Roy survived, and I have photos of them dancing on the veranda & of me swimming in a water hole on the property. Yerba Buena also had a big aviary with all sorts of birds. We also had a spider monkey called Maria who used to take hold of Nevile's pram & walk him with mummy! LOL. Mummy told me that she believes the cook poisoned Maria because Maria would empty bags of flour all over the kitchen.*

*Mummy had a great love for animals & flowering plants, which I believe she passed on to me. Our family left for Jamaica when all of us were still small. Our parents lived the high life there as Roy played polo & ran H.E. Robinson, a company selling Rover cars & other makes. I don't recall if that's the exact name of the company. The British cricket team stayed at our house whenever they came to Jamaica; the team included Sir Leonard Hutton & Sir Godfrey Evans. I remember joking around with them & taking pictures with my brownie camera which often didn't have any film in it!*

*We had a gorgeous home called Sharrow which had a stable at the bottom of the very long driveway leading up to the house. The stable had polo ponies & a racehorse called Beaverbrook after Lord Beaverbrook the British publishing magnate. The Main house was large & white with a large circular staircase leading up to the top floor, quite grand, & reminded me of the estate in "Gone with the Wind", very ante bellum in style.*

*My parents were often invited to Government House by the Governor of Jamaica, Sir Hugh Foot, & would often take us with them. I clearly remember Alice, the Princess of Athlone, dangling me on her knees on her visits.*

# Chapter 4 Part 2 – Maternal Aunts and Uncles

*In those days, the Queen & Prince Philip would visit the island. Daddy provided all the land rovers for their parades through Kingston etc. Daddy played polo with the Duke of Edinburgh, & they were invited to dine on the royal yacht "Britannia". All of this is true as I have saved letters to my father from Sir Hugh Foot thanking him for all his help etc. We used to have the royal coat of arms emblems in our home but with all of the moving from country to country they've disappeared.*

*At this time in Jamaica were such luminaries as Sir Ian Fleming, Errol Flynn, and influxes of well-known visitors from all over the world. My parents met them all including Vivien Leigh & her then husband Sir Laurence Olivier.*

*Lord & Lady Glenconnor also visited us. Lord Glenconnor (the family name was Tennant, Lord & Lady Glenconnor titles). They were called Ernest & Irene Tennant. Their son Colin Tenant was known for entertaining Princess Margaret on his island of Mustique. He inherited the family title, & was apparently very odd, I learned from later sources. Mummy & Daddy went to his wedding in London, a very grand occasion.*

*There were many more adventures & characters in Jamaica, not all of whose names I can remember. Nevile & I were sent to stay with Count & Countess Mowcowski (sic) a Polish couple with a magnificent estate outside Montego Bay when Mummy went to England for a visit. I believe she was considering divorcing Daddy due to his affair with his coloured secretary, Miss Evans. Obviously, she didn't go through with this. We had a grand time with this very grand couple & their two children. The count taught me to ride side-saddle in a long skirt, & to jump as well!!! I was only 10.*

*We left Jamaica for England when I was 10 & Nevile was 8 with mummy, Roy must have flown. Clive was a pupil at St. Edwards in Oxford already. We took a banana boat from Jamaica. It was the Elder & Fyffe (sic) line. Uncle Milton must have been visiting as he drove us in a truck with all our luggage, & I think our three dogs. I don't know where he took the dogs, but I remember he was very*

89

# From Barbados to Banffshire

*skinny & sweet, although he did drive us off the road. Milton (I believe it was Milton), managed to get us back on the road in time to board our ship. When we arrived, it was fascinating to see a long line of Jamaican men with huge bunches of bananas queueing up to load the ship. So, the calypso was acted out right in front of our eyes! I remember it every time Harry Belafonte sings his song. We had a very pleasant voyage, but I missed Jamaica, the dogs, the friends, especially our nanny Miss Millicent Tate whom we loved very much. I really think Mummy was happiest in Jamaica with all the parties & big life with both the famous & the infamous.*

*Nevile (Alec) & I still talk about the time our dear parents left us to go to a party knowing that there was a hurricane warning. We survived the hurricane by jimmying open Clive's locked side table with all his comics & reading them! All the servants fled, & the horses got out of the stable. The house was huge & old, trees came. crashing down around us, & the bottom floor flooded. Somewhere we found rubber boots which we used to navigate the flooding. We must have found a flashlight as well. We loved the whole thing. Eventually the two showed up having to leave their chauffeured car way down the driveway due to a huge tree having crashed right in front of their rover. I know there are many more stories to be told about our time in Jamaica."*

Daphne moved around quite a bit after marrying Roy Simpson. Their children settled quite far apart too. Clive moved to live in Australia. His two children are now grown up. His son Grant has three young sons and works as an estate agent in Australia. Clive's daughter, Greta, also works in real estate in Australia. I am in touch with her through Instagram. Clive died in 2018, his wife Beverley Anne having died much earlier, in 1985, due to an embolism when she was only 40 years old.

Lois and her brother Alec Nevile Simpson MD, live at opposite sides of the USA. Lois is an art and design graduate, who is still involved in the high-end fashion business. Dave and I visited Lois and her husband Philip in their beautiful home in San Francisco in 2017. We had a lovely time.

# Chapter 4 Part 2 – Maternal Aunts and Uncles

Nevile is a retired vascular surgeon of some repute in New Jersey. Nevile is known as Alec Simpson to all except his close family. Dave and I stayed with Nevile and his first wife Karin in New Jersey in 1994. They have one son, Joel, whom we first met when he was only five years old. We subsequently met him as an adult at a family wedding in Scotland in 2009. Karin sadly died of lung cancer at the age of 43. She had never been a smoker and lived a very healthy lifestyle, so it was a great shock to learn that she had contracted that life-threatening illness. We liked Karin very much. Using his medical knowledge, Nevile tried desperately to find a cure for his wife. Karin tragically died in the year 2000 approximately one year after contracting the disease. Nevile has since remarried and found happiness again.

I met Uncle Roy when our families had a "Turpin Reunion" in 1992 here in Scotland. At that time, they were debating whether to leave Panama, where they lived at that time, and move to the USA. When I asked him what he wanted to do, he replied "*Stay in Panama of course, I prefer to be a big fish in a small pond rather than a small fish in a big pond like the U.S.*"

Roy died in Panama City on 12th March 1995. at the age of 89. Auntie Daphne moved to Florida not long afterwards. She suffered from osteoarthritis in her later years like her father and her sisters. Daphne died following a stroke in Warren, New Jersey on 21st May 2004. She was almost 87 years old.

**James Edmund <u>Michael</u> Turpin born on 23rd November 1921**

Uncle Michael born in Barbados, was my mother's oldest brother and was christened James Edmund Michael Turpin. He was known as Michael within the family. He spent his childhood in British Guiana and was educated at Queens College, Georgetown.

According to a Guyana newspaper cutting dated 17th January 1946, he left home in 1937 and joined the Grenadier Guards in London:

# From Barbados to Banffshire

*"He saw service in France and Belgium from September 1939 to June 1940. He later served in the Armoured Division of the Guards and remained with it until 1942. In 1945 he was awarded the Military Cross during operations in Burma. He attended Royal Military College in 1943 and was promoted to 2nd Lieutenant and subsequently posted to the Queens Own Royal West Kent Regiment. In 1943 he volunteered for special service and served with the S.R. unit of Small Operation Group and later was engaged in experimental work in California and the Bahamas. In 1944 he qualified as a parachutist. He was then promoted to the rank of Captain in the British Army and posted to Ceylon (Sri Lanka)".*

Mum told us that Uncle Michael lied about his age when he was 17 years old because he wanted to go to England and join the war effort in 1939. My mother was very proud to tell us that he was awarded the Military Cross for bravery. The following is a citation which can be found online and details the operations which lead to Uncle Michael receiving the Military Cross.

**Lieutenant James Edmund Michael Turpin 265889**
**No.4 Section S.R.U. Royal West Kent Regiment**
**Military Cross (WO-373-40-23) Burma March 1945**

*Lieut. Turpin was a member of No. 4 Sec SRU which was under command of 5th Infantry Brigade for the three weeks prior to and during the actual operation resulting in the establishment of a bridgehead on the South bank of the Irrawaddy River in the Myittha area on 24/25th February 1945.*
*Owing to the strong current and shifting sandbars it was extremely difficult to find suitable crossing places and this section of the SRU carried out no less than eight separate night reconnaissances in order to obtain the required information.*

92

# Chapter 4 Part 2 – Maternal Aunts and Uncles

*Lieut. Turpin took part in six of these eight reconnaissances. Under the eyes of the enemy, he succeeded in charting the sandbanks, testing the depth of the water, gauging the effect of the current on assault craft and obtaining definite information regarding possible landing beaches. Without this information it would have been extremely difficult to decide upon the best crossing places and the most suitable methods to employ.*

*In addition to the above reconnaissances Lt. Turpin organised and carried out an extremely successful diversionary raid on Letpantabin on the night 11th February 1945.*

*On the night of the actual crossing Lt. Turpin, assisted by Sgt. Colgan, led the first flight of the 1 RWF across to Ngazun Island. They found barbed wire along the bank but cut gaps in it to allow the assault craft to get through.*

*The first boats arrived safely but the enemy then opened up on the beach and Lt. Turpin gave valuable assistance in collection of the wounded, improvising beach lights and guiding the craft, all under fire.*

*At 0400 hrs an approaching boat was sunk by enemy fire and the occupants were thrown out on to a sandbank 500 yards from the shore. Lt. Turpin swam out to this sandbank, collected a wounded man, and swam back with him to the shore. He then swam out again and guided the unwounded men to safety.*

*At 0550 hrs Lt. Turpin swam across to the North Bank, collected medical supplies which were urgently required by the bridgehead, and with Sgt. Colgan brought them safely across.*

*Later Lt. Turpin, assisted by Sgt. Colgan and one RE, lashed three boats together and succeeded in ferrying some seriously wounded men across to the North bank.*

*All these exploits were carried out by Lt. Turpin under heavy fire and with magnificent disregard for his own safety.*

*His sustained efforts and achievements inspired everyone in the bridgehead, and he contributed in no small way to the success of a very difficult operation.*

Uncle Michael's wife Phoebe told me of the existence of the above citation and that he received the Military Cross only a day after the operations described above were completed. These escapades are

# From Barbados to Banffshire

also mentioned in a book called "The Frogmen of Burma" by Bruce S. Wright, as well as a book called "Undercover Sailors" by A.Cecil Hampshire. These books are still available online.

After the war ended, Michael decided to become a tea planter in Assam, India. I only met him once when he brought Phoebe to visit us in our home at Crossroads Farm, Rothiemay. My sisters and I were spellbound and in awe of this very handsome, tall (6ft 4in) young man who came to stay for a few days. He towered above his petite, pretty wife, Phoebe. We were fascinated as he recounted (under pressure to do so by us schoolgirls) some of his escapades during his wartime experiences. He was not proud of having had to kill enemy soldiers but told us "*It was a case of kill or be killed*".

Another story I do remember from his visit (I was ten years old at the time) was of his experience of having to hunt and kill a man-eating tiger, which had killed and eaten one of the workmen on the tea plantation he managed after the war. This was in Assam, India. He had been wakened up by the workers on the plantation and they pleaded with him to go with them and kill the tiger before it killed someone else. We were spellbound listening to him as he was a very good storyteller.

We never saw him again sadly as he died of a heart attack in Worthing at the age of 49 on 14th April 1971 just after retiring to England. His death was particularly sad for my mother as it happened only a few weeks after my father had died on 26th March that same year.

Mum told us that she had dreamed of him the night before she received the news. He had been standing at the foot of her bed wearing a white night gown looking just like she remembered him as a young boy with golden curls. She was very calm telling us the news and said she did not get a shock when the news came of his death. She had been expecting it, because of the dream. Mum had not been aware that he was ill at that time. It was all very sudden and sad for all the family, but it must have been particularly hard for his wife and children.

# Chapter 4 Part 2 – Maternal Aunts and Uncles

I was in touch with Phoebe in 2009 when she kindly bought six copies of my son David's poetry book "Flying My Own Plane". She had kept in touch with my mother regularly until Mum died in 2008. We lost touch after 2010 but after finding a card amongst Mum's papers, which Phoebe had sent my mother some time ago, I phoned the number. I was delighted when she answered the phone and am happy to say she sounds as bright as ever. She does have some health problems being 92 years old but is still able to live in her own house. My most recent information is that Phoebe is now bedridden and has carers in to look after her. She is still cheerful and enjoys family visits.

It has been wonderful to have some long chats with Phoebe on the phone and I'm so glad she was able to help me ensure that the information I have written about Uncle Michael was correct.

Michael and Phoebe had three children, Raine, Toni Jane. and Simon. Phoebe and the children returned to England to live near Phoebe's parents, Mr and Mrs Langford Ray so that the children could be educated there. Michael travelled from India to England to see them as often as possible.

Raine was born on 8th January 1950. She married Richard Wells in 1970 in Worthing, Sussex. They had two children, Leona and Ruaridh, who live in England. Raine sadly died in Lambeth, London in August 1991 when she was only 41. She had lived for a time in New Zealand, so my New Zealand cousins got to know her while she was there. Leona lives not far from Phoebe and visits her regularly. I met Toni Jane when she came up to Aberdeenshire to visit my mother. Toni and her husband Robert live in England. They have one daughter and one grandson.

I have never met Simon but spoke to him on the phone recently when he was visiting his mother Phoebe. Simon has one daughter, Emily, who has two children. Simon has retired from working in the property business in Dubai. He also spent some time working in China. He was divorced from his first wife six years ago and is now happily remarried and lives in Devon.

# From Barbados to Banffshire

## Christine Maud Eyre Turpin was born on 15th June 1926

Auntie Christine was born in British Guiana when her father was Canon of St Saviour's Church, Fort Wellington. She was the youngest daughter of my grandparents, Milton and Constance Turpin.

Grandpa Turpin adored his youngest daughter. His "pet" name for her was "Sweet Lavender". My mother told us that this was because when she was born, her mother used to place lavender sachets in her cot, possibly to deter flies. Grandpa used to remark on how sweetly she smelled.

According to information I have received from her daughters, Pamela, Margaret and Carole, their mother left her home in British Guiana in 1941 at the age of 16 years after contracting malaria. She travelled on a troop ship that was blacked out because of the war. She went to stay with her Uncle Charles Vivian Turpin in Trinidad. There she convalesced and eventually obtained work with the United States Forces in an administrative capacity.

Soon afterwards she met and fell in love with Sub Lieutenant Commander John Carpenter, a New Zealander. They were married in Trinidad and the beautiful young bride was given away by her Uncle Charles. **Christine is pictured left on her wedding day**.

When the war ended, Mr and Mrs John Carpenter together with their young baby Pamela, moved to New Zealand to live in John's home city of Auckland. Uncle John brought Auntie Christine to Scotland to visit us at the farm when I was a child. He loved to tell jokes and tease us girls. I remember Mum telling us that when the Queen came to New Zealand to visit the country, Christine and John were presented to the royal couple

# Chapter 4 Part 2 – Maternal Aunts and Uncles

when they arrived in Auckland. Uncle John was a prominent businessman in Auckland at the time.

Their son Byron was born soon after their arrival in New Zealand. He was a good looking, clever young man who died tragically at the age of 21 years. This caused extreme sadness in the family especially for his mother who my mother believed never got over the loss. However, I think her resilience and positive attitude which seems to run in our family helped her to cope with the unbearable loss. Auntie Christine hid her sorrow and continued to be the cheerful, inspirational mother loved by her three daughters and her grand children.

In 1977 Christine's second daughter Margaret (known as Margie) married Amir Rad, an Iranian businessman. His business took him to the USA where they lived in San Antonio until they retired back to New Zealand. Their daughter Sara, her brother Cyrus and Margie's two sisters Pamela and Carole still live in New Zealand. Margie had qualified in the USA as a Drug & Alcohol Counsellor, work she found to be both inspiring and rewarding. I am in touch with her regularly through Facebook. Pamela is divorced and Carole is a widow. They both live in Auckland. Carole's children Matthew, Joanna and their families live in the Auckland area.

Margie has sent me some memories which she and her sisters remember their mother Christine telling them. She told them about my mother Margot being a teacher to Christine and her younger siblings. They did not have mod cons in the vicarage. The housekeeper would boil water and fill up a big tub for them to take baths. The house was next door to a sugarcane plantation. There were snakes around in the nearby waters, so she never learned to swim. They had no electricity, just kerosene lamps.

These stories were similar to the stories my mother told us. However, Mum and Daphne must have learned to swim when they went to Trinidad to receive their education. As children growing up in Scotland with its cool summers and freezing winters, we used to love getting Auntie Christine's letters and photos from Auckland.

# From Barbados to Banffshire

The children looked so happy surrounded by beautiful flowers in a sun-drenched garden, dressed in lovely summer clothes. We were very envious.

Auntie Christine was beautiful "inside and out", of that there is no doubt. She had the most wonderful soprano voice which she managed to maintain at least until she was well into her eighties. Dave and I were fortunate to be able to visit her and meet her daughters and their families in 2010. At that time, she was 85 years old, and she was happy to let us video her singing her favourite songs such as "Let Me Call You Sweetheart", "Red Sails in the Sunset" and "I Could Have Danced All Night". It has given me immense pleasure to be able to share these videos on Facebook to the delight of many of our friends and relatives who have seen them. Christine said she used to entertain the troops during the war and enjoyed singing in church. I was delighted to meet her having only met her briefly on some of her very infrequent visits to my mother in Scotland.

This is a lovely story from her daughter Margie:

*"Mum told us she used to sing "Alice Blue Gown" to the troops on many occasions. As shy as she was, her singing gave her great confidence. Sometimes she would break into song in a restaurant when she heard a song she knew and we as children would want to hide under the table; but were really secretly very proud amid all the clapping from the people there."*

Auntie Christine's delightfully uncomplaining personality seemed to help her maintain her positive attitude throughout the difficulties she experienced. She reminded me quite a lot of my mother who had died in 2008. It was comforting to be in her company as I found her mannerisms were very similar to my mother's. They were obviously very close in spite of the age difference of about seven years. They corresponded frequently by air mail letters when separated by thousands of miles.

# Chapter 4 Part 2 – Maternal Aunts and Uncles

Uncle John died in 1981 after a sudden heart attack. As much as he was her rock in life from a very early age, we were all pleased she was able to find happiness again in her second marriage to Australian Reginald Taylor. They left New Zealand to live in Perth, Western Australia when they got married. My mother enjoyed her visit to them there in 1987.

Christine returned to live in Auckland after her husband Reg died. Christine died aged 89 years on 15th February 2014 after a period of ill health, her stoic and positive attitude continuing to the end. A sad loss for all of us who knew her. I know this may sound silly but when I'm singing hymns in church and there are high notes, I imagine she is with me, and I can reach those notes!

**Milton Everett Andrew Turpin was born on 26th June 1926**

Uncle Milton born in British Guiana, was the second oldest son of my grandparents Milton and Connie Turpin. He was the second youngest member of the family of seven children. He spent his childhood in British Guiana and was educated there. My mother used to tell us some very amusing stories about her brother Milton growing up. He loved to play with the local children of his age, and he used to come home covered in mud from their escapades. She also told us that when his big sister Daphne started courting, and she was expecting a potential suitor to call, Milton would often arrive home looking very scruffy and dirty. Auntie Daphne used to put him in a cupboard leaving strict instructions with their mother and whoever was there that on no account was Milton to be allowed out of the cupboard until the potential suitor had escorted her from the premises.

Mum also told us that to make some pocket money, Milton would offer his skills as a photographer specialising in wedding photography to the local residents of the parish. On one occasion he forgot to put the film in the camera with the resulting deep disappointment experienced by the wedding party. Somehow or other he had the kind of face and charm which allowed him to get away with this without suffering too many consequences.

# From Barbados to Banffshire

My sisters and I adored Uncle Milton and looked forward very much to his visits to us at Crossroads Farm. He told us some very amusing stories of his young life in British Guiana and as an adult in England. He was a self-professed agnostic and used to like to disagree with my mother's rather idealistic view of life, but did so in a very humorous way, which usually made her laugh at herself. I recall him telling me about his tasks as a choir boy to his father, holding the holy water and fetching and carrying for him. He did not nurse any ambitions to follow his father and grandfather into the ministry of the Anglican Church.

When Milton was still quite young, he liked to practise for his future vocation, which was to become an engineer. He set himself up as a clock fixer and persuaded people to part with their clocks which had stopped working for one reason or another. Unsuspecting neighbours and friends of the family would hand in their clocks to the vicarage where he lived (he was the parson's son so what could possibly go wrong)! While he was very good at dismantling the clocks, he rarely managed to put them back together again. He would hide when the people came to collect their still silent clocks. Milton did train as an engineer and worked all his life in that profession, but I don't think he specialised in clocks.

Uncle Milton travelled to England in 1948 to train as an engineer. He started work in a foundry in Derby and met and married Edna Eley in 1952. Milton and Edna had three children, Linda, Fay, and Milton.

**Milton and Edna Turpin**

# Chapter 4 Part 2 – Maternal Aunts and Uncles

Not long after Linda was born, they emigrated to Jamaica where Milton got work as an engineer in the sugar industry. Fay and Milton were both born in Jamaica. Fay told me she has no memory of Jamaica as they returned to Derby when she was only 2 years old in 1958. Uncle Milton told us that Edna had been very unhappy with the climate and lifestyle out there and she missed her family dreadfully. Her mental health deteriorated, and she developed chronic agoraphobia, which caused her to start drinking alcohol to overcome her unhappiness. Because Edna was so unhappy and missing her family in England, Milton felt he had no option but to return to Derby with the family.

While they were living in Jamaica, he used to send us parcels of West Indian delicacies such as guava cheese which I can still remember as one of my very favourite tastes. My father used to say that we were "like hens among corn" when these parcels arrived.

My sisters and I were able to spend more time getting to know Uncle Milton when the family moved back to England from Jamaica. I remember their first visit to the farm on their return to the UK. Their children were very small.

Uncle Milton and his youngest brother Guy both had strong Guyanese accents, having lived all their young lives in British Guiana. He told us that when he and his family returned to England, they had difficulty finding a house to live in. However, when he eventually decided to call at the estate agent's office in person, without making an appointment, he had no problem. He realised that when he phoned to ask for a viewing, the reason he was told the house was unavailable was because his Guyanese accent made him sound Black. 1950's Britain was very racist.

Uncle Milton was a very capable, dependable human being and parent. He had a difficult life being the main carer for his children while holding down a full-time job. Edna never recovered from her agoraphobia, and she continued to use alcohol in a more dependent way than she would have wanted to. The couple divorced, and while the children continued to spend some happy

# From Barbados to Banffshire

times with their mother, when she was well, Uncle Milton had to be the main carer for the children. Eventually he found happiness with his second wife Gwen, and they were married in 1977. By that time, the children were teenagers and Linda had a daughter of her own. Edna sadly died in March 1978 at the age of 48.

Milton did bring Gwen to Scotland to visit us sometimes, but she did not enjoy our Scottish climate, so latterly, when he visited us he was on his own. We always enjoyed his visits and he and my mother were very close. They both loved to dance and, sometimes during his visits, we would have house parties with music and dancing. The amusing stories were ever present at every visit. It was a case of "the way you tell them". We were all very sad when he became ill with cancer in 2007. Dave and I visited him a few days before he died. He was remarkably cheerful, considering he was so ill. We got a shock when we were told he had died on 26th August 2007 so soon after our visit. He was 81 years old.

Milton has left behind several grandchildren and great grandchildren as well as Linda, Fay, and Milton. Although we had only minimal contact with them, due to geographical constraints, I feel very fortunate to have been able to make their acquaintance quite recently via Facebook and see the photos of their children and grandchildren. I can see Uncle Milton's mischievous smile and whimsical eyes shining out from this photo of his small great grandsons. (Fay's grandchildren), sons of Laurie. This is very heart warming and does seem to keep his memory alive in a lovely way.

**Charlie and Harrison**

# Chapter 4 Part 2 – Maternal Aunts and Uncles

## Guy Oswald Garnet Turpin was born on 26th September 1931

Uncle Guy also born in British Guiana, was the youngest of my mother's siblings. His brother Milton was 5 years old when he was born and they were very close.

Guy was a quiet, good natured wee boy according to some relatives and just played around the area with the local children picking up the very strong Guyanese accent which we enjoyed listening to whenever we met him.

Uncle Guy used to write letters to my mother regularly from wherever he was living. He had very artistic handwriting. I remember reading his letters as a child and liking the way he would put the word (smiles) in brackets after telling my mother about something he thought she would find amusing. No emojis in those days. He enjoyed painting and used to send my mother very colourful paintings for her birthdays. (See painting of house in Guyana on this book's back cover).

As previously said in her own story, Guy's mother Connie suffered from alcohol addiction, which caused her health to deteriorate. This must have been very difficult for Guy growing up, but he never spoke about it to us or his children as far as I know. She died suddenly, collapsing in her bathroom from a heart attack in March 1949. Guy told his family that it was he who experienced the trauma of being the one to find her. Guy would have been about 18 years old. He had just started work as an overseer on a sugar plantation but told his father and Aunt Stella that he did not like giving people orders so did not work there for long.

Grandpa Turpin suffered from osteoarthritis and experienced difficulty walking, so his sister Stella came to stay with them to offer support. The rest of the family had left home, including Milton who

# From Barbados to Banffshire

had sailed for England on 27th July 1948 to train as an engineer. Daphne and Roy left for Jamaica about the same time. Guy left his job as an overseer and returned home on 18th March 1950. In her letters to her daughter Sheila, Stella makes comments about Guy becoming very lethargic and inactive. "He sits around all day just eating all the food," she writes. I believe this was an obvious symptom of a young man very depressed at the loss of his mother. In those days people suffering from depression would not get much sympathy as it would not be recognised as the very common illness it is today.

Guy did seek work in other types of employment in the West Indian islands without success. With the encouragement of his brother Milton who had settled in the Derby area, Guy decided to look for work in the UK. He boarded a ship bound for England from Trinidad on the 10th of October 1951. His father, in a letter to his sister Stella, describes how worried he was that he had no word from Milton or Guy to say he had arrived safely. Milton became concerned as well when no word was received by 30th October. He contacted the shipping agents to inquire why "The Pantha", the ship Guy was a passenger on, had not yet arrived in England. The agents told him that the delay was due to the "Pantha" having to tow another ship which was in distress. The ship was having to dock in Cornwall then make its way to Cardiff. Grandpa was relieved that Milton had been able to get this information. He was clearly very concerned for Guy. He eventually received a telegram from Milton to say Guy had arrived safely on 11th November. "*This news relieves me of much anxiety*", Grandpa writes. Milton helped Guy to look for employment in England. Guy eventually joined the RAF as a gunner.

From 1952 until Guy got married in 1958, we got to know him very well as he used to come to the farm on his leave from the RAF. My sisters and I fell madly in love with him and he was great fun. He would take us to the cinema and go on long walks with us. Margaret loved art and was very good at it. Uncle Guy would take Margaret and I out sketching or painting landmarks in the neighbourhood. I was hopeless at art but pretended I wasn't to get to accompany them. My most vivid memory of this is of sitting in a ditch painting a church not far from home. I have nothing to show for my efforts.

We looked forward very much to Uncle Guy coming to stay for about three weeks at a time, when on leave from the RAF. Dad had hoped Uncle Guy could be one of his farm workers when he came to the farm on leave from the RAF. Mum insisted that her brother should not be doing farm work from dawn to dusk and should be free to spend time with us children when we were not at school. Dad grudgingly agreed to this. Farmers don't see any merit in an able-bodied man having leisure time when there is work to be done on the farm.

I loved to hear Guy sing. He sounded like Bing Crosby or Perry Como and would sing loudly while shaving or having a bath. I have some recordings of him singing on tape with his daughter Connie when they came over to visit us in Scotland in 1992. She has a lovely voice too. Uncle Guy's son Milton has a rich tone to his voice and has sung professionally. He sounded quite like his father when I heard him at a family wedding in Ireland.

We were selfishly disappointed when our fun uncle met his wife Sally in Ireland and his visits stopped. Sally's maiden name was Guy interestingly enough; can you imagine their first conversation? Uncle Guy was obviously happy to have met her, so we were happy for him but very jealous. His oldest daughter Lucinda gave me the following information. Her parents met at a dance in Limavady, Northern Ireland. They got married in Limavady on 7th February 1958. Sally was a member of a large Irish Catholic family. They had a double wedding with Sally's sister Frances. Before they got married, Guy had to change his religion to Catholicism and attended lessons so that he could be accepted into that faith. He was confirmed by the Bishop of Derry and Sally's brother Brian was his sponsor. All of Sally's family were very fond of Guy, and he of them. He left the RAF after injuring his leg and started work with a German firm based 3 miles from Limavady.

# From Barbados to Banffshire

Sally and Guy had six children. Jude was born in 1960, Milton in 1962, Lucinda in 1963, Connie in 1965, Mary in 1967 and Grace in 1970. Sally sadly died in 1985, when Grace was only fifteen. The children are all alive and well. Jude is still single, but all the others are married and there are numerous grandchildren. Guy's granddaughters are all very beautiful. His grandsons are a credit to their parents and grandparents. Dave and I have attended two Irish weddings which were very enjoyable. We have always received excellent hospitality when visiting; the "craic" is always good.

The IRA troubles in Northern Ireland were a worrying time for the family. In 1968 before we realised how much the violence had escalated, my first husband Norman and I took our very young children, David and Pamela, to visit my sister Margaret and her new husband Patrick in Portadown. We then drove the 70 miles to Limavady to see Guy, Sally and their family. We were shocked to see that numerous small fires were burning on the road to Belfast. It was like a war zone. This was quite hazardous as the car had to be driven very carefully in between burning tyres on the main road.

The family (being Catholic) were experiencing discrimination from the ruling Protestant government. They had been hoping to move to a bigger house but were constantly disappointed. No sooner had they been informed they were at the top of the list, when they found out the house, they had expected to get had been allocated to Protestant tenants. The cleansing department were refusing to collect the bins from the Catholic families when we were there, and the unrest was obviously quite intolerable at times. We found the family to be quite happy go lucky and uncomplaining when we visited. Sally had gone to a lot of trouble to serve a lovely meal for us. Although it did not happen for some years after our visit, it was a great relief for us all when the Peace Agreement was signed in 1998, and the unrest and fighting ceased.

# Chapter 4 Part 2 – Maternal Aunts and Uncles

Lucinda takes up the story here, talking about her father:

*"His favourite film was "To Kill a Mockingbird", and he first watched it in the cinema with his mother. His dad was very strict, and I remember him telling me the story about him scheming off school to go swimming in the river. Unfortunately, he cut his leg on a piece of tin but didn't tell his dad lol. He also told me he caught malaria when he was young and that his dad nursed him back to health giving him Coca Cola. He always maintained the coke of our generation was not the same.*

*He loved his pipe and he was mad about Laurel and Hardy. I bought him the complete collection of them on DVD but it was his hearty laugh that made us laugh. He loved painting but he also loved making things. When Mum died my son, Martin, was almost two and Dad took on the role of minding him while I worked. I remember coming home from work to find him pulling Martin on a go cart he had made him, on the front street. He also made a massive, big bow and arrow and would go out the back and shoot arrows at the bullseye he had made. When we were younger during the troubles, he never allowed the boys to have toy guns as he was scared they would be mistaken for real ones.*

*When I was younger, Dad would take me up the town every Saturday morning, and we would go to a wee cafe and he would have coffee and I would have a bun. Dad would speak to anyone he met even if he didn't know them and would call all the men Pat, why I don't know.*

*He hated Irish stew and was never keen on home made soup but I'm sure you know he loved curry. lol."*

Uncle Guy's health deteriorated as he aged and Jude became his carer. As he became more disabled, extra help had to be provided by social services. All of us were very sad when he died on 26th November 2016 in hospital in Limavady.

# From Barbados to Banffshire

## Guyana Holiday 1993

Dave and I visited Guyana in 1993 when the country was less politically unstable than it had been for some time. When we travelled to Venezuela for Dave's work in 1989, we had enquired about visiting Guyana, but the British Embassy advised against it due to the political instability there. As we discovered, Venezuela was not that peaceful either as when we were in Caracas, we could hear gunshots ringing out through the night and were advised not to leave our hotel after dark.

Guyana had gained political independence from Britain in 1966. No political party had been able to lift Guyana out of poverty and the political unrest due to corruption and fraudulent elections throughout the country continued until 1992. The elections held that year were considered to be fair and free by the international community. Cheddi Jagan, who had led the country prior to independence was voted back in. Due to information detailing that the situation had stabilised, we felt reassured that it would be safe to visit the country.

When we arrived, it was like stepping into 1950's Britain. The infrastructure was poor. Roads were not maintained and the cars were very reminiscent of that decade. When we asked which side of the road they drive on, our taxi driver told us "*Whatever side has no potholes*". We hardly saw any white people but locals were friendly. When passing any of the local men, they saluted Dave and addressed him "*White Chief*"!: more than a hint of sarcasm, of course, but we found it amusing as well as embarrassing.

We were advised that before the political situation settled, visitors were advised not to wear scarves or ties and not to carry expensive handbags or wear jewellery for fear of being robbed in the street. There was a café in the main street called "The Choke and Rob". We gave it a wide berth and I was careful not to wear a scarf.

The Guyanese people seem to have quite a sense of humour don't you think?

# Chapter 4 Part 2 – Maternal Aunts and Uncles

Dave adds the following observations:

*"Georgetown is built on the tidal exposed mudflats of the Demerara River estuary. In case of flooding many of the buildings are made with wood and built on stilts. St George's Cathedral is well worth a visit. Built from various species and colours of hardwood (including greenheart) transported from the Guyana rainforest, the building is reputed to be the tallest church built only from wood, in the world.*

*When travelling along Georgetown's seaside we noticed a number of large cast iron sluice gates. We were told that these gates were built and maintained by the British in colonial days. The gates had allowed the seawater to enter the town and fill the canals at the side of the streets. The gates were shut at high tide and all the litter from the town was deposited into the canals. The sluice gates were then opened at low tide thereby allowing the pent-up water and rubbish behind to rush out into the sea. A very practical idea for the time. However, when Guyana became independent and the British left, the sluice gates were left to rust solid, and the canals could no longer be flushed. There was a lot of litter in Georgetown when we visited".*

We had contacted the British Embassy in Georgetown as well as the Diocese office of the Anglican church of St George's Cathedral. They arranged for us to meet with the Bishop of Guyana for an informal meeting. We had expected a very stately, much older gentleman and were surprised to be greeted by a pleasant young man dressed in shorts and brightly coloured tee shirt. He was introduced to us as "Bishop George" and apologised for his casual attire saying he was about to go away on a retreat with fellow preachers and "his team".He remembered having been a choirboy in my grandfather's church and remembered "the Turpin boys" who had also been choir boys before him. We found him to be a friendly informal man with a wonderful booming baritone speaking voice.

The next visit we had prearranged was a visit to the sugar company which my father had worked for when in Guyana called Booker Brothers, now known as "Guysuco". Bearing in mind our family had

# From Barbados to Banffshire

left Guyana for good in 1947, we were impressed that they had taken the trouble to look back into records of my father's employment with them and had located photos of my father in groups with other managers and overseers. We were pleasantly surprised when they told us they had assigned a chauffeur and an additional minder to drive us wherever we wanted to go.

One of the places I wanted to see was Bartica to see where Grandpa had been a newly qualified priest and where Aunt Grace was born. I had promised her we would visit there and tell her about it. Our obliging minders took us to where we could board a passenger speed boat to take us up the Essequibo River to Bartica. It was an exhilarating trip and being the only white passengers, we were treated like VIPs. We felt a bit embarrassed when we were ushered on to the front seats in the boat after the people already occupying those seats had been rather rudely told to move.

The town of Bartica reminded me of a wild west station in a cowboy film. The houses were mostly just shacks; the roads were dirt tracks. Accommodation was hard to find. We booked into the only hotel in Bartica but. when we realised that it was a brothel, we quickly cancelled our night's accommodation there. The nearest toilet was at the end of a long corridor some distance from our allocated bedroom!

When we ventured in to the "town" we were shown where to buy gold jewellery, almost secretively, from under the counter in a small shop selling leather goods. A young man befriended us in the street and took us to a bar where we were entertained by large rats skipping along a ledge above our heads. I can't remember what I had to drink. He took us to a bed and breakfast place which must go down in my experience as the worst accommodation I've ever attempted to sleep in. The heat and mosquitos were relentless. We only had one single sheet between the two of us. The toilet facilities were out of order, and the stench was quite horrible. The couple in the next room were very noisy, possibly on honeymoon? When they went to sleep the donkeys began their courting. "Hee-haw" sang out loudly for what seemed like ages. It was a relief to give up trying to sleep and go downstairs for a breakfast of fried eggs which we enjoyed. The landlady was very pleasant. Our "friend" came back next day and asked us to pay for his company and help in finding accommodation. We had only a very few Guyanese dollars with us, and he was not very happy with the 5 dollars we gave him. We were very glad to get back to the comparative luxury of our accommodation in Georgetown.

According to a Guyanese Facebook friend, Bartica is now quite an upmarket place to visit with some lovely houses and well maintained streets. However, there are still a number of brothels in the town.

We were also able to visit the plantation I had lived on in Demerara, but the house we lived in had been demolished soon after we left for Scotland. It was pouring with warm rain. Undeterred I told our guide that I wanted to find the garden where my sister and I had played in a sandpit under a palm tree. We did find the garden according to our guide but when I asked him if the palm tree I remembered was still there, he pointed out a headless trunk, saying with great authority, "*That's it... but de top come off.*"

Dekinderen, the sugar plantation where we had lived, had been absorbed into the much larger plantation of Uigfluct. We were taken to meet the manager in his office. He invited us to have lunch in his home where his wife treated us to a lovely meal with lots of fresh fruit. The house was palatial and the garden beautiful and well-tended.

Mum had suggested we ask to be taken to meet a man called Steve, a man in his 60's who had been only 17 when my parents lived there. He was of mixed ethnicity. Mum had suggested we seek him out and told us they knew his father who was Scottish. Steve was the sandwich boy on the plantation when we had lived there. He lived in a small shack with a galvanised roof. The rain battered the roof and was quite deafening. He said he remembered "*the parson*" as well as my parents. He served us tea in tin mugs and seemed very pleased to see us.

# From Barbados to Banffshire

The next day we booked a plane journey to the Kaietur Falls which was the most amazing sight I have ever seen. The Falls are reputed to have the largest single drop volume of water of any waterfall in the world. The roar was deafening and really exciting. There were no safety barriers or restaurants. The plane was very small, seating only 6 people and seemed quite dilapidated. Landing and taking off on the wet slippery, muddy landing strip offered another exciting experience. We did get there and back in one piece to our great surprise and relief. The colour insert photograph of the Kaeitur Falls was taken by me. Dave is the person perched on the ledge beside the falls holding microphones and making a stereo recording of the roar of the falls on a tape recorder. We still have it somewhere.

Guyana is a beautiful country with rich resources, such as gold, bauxite and more recently oil. The country continues to have intermittent periods of unrest which has made it difficult for us to plan a return journey. However, Guyana has been listed online as one of the fastest growing economies in the Western World.

# Section 2
# To Banffshire, Scotland

# From Barbados to Banffshire

**My Father's Grandparents were Alexander Weir (1832 - 1908) and Jane Forsyth (1842 - 1930).**

They farmed at Clerkseat, Grange, Banffshire and my great grandfather Alexander Weir died there in 1908. His wife Jane also died there, 22 years later.

Jane Forsyth was born in Achairn, Keith to Elspet Turner and William Forsyth. Elspet died in 1861 at the age of 45. Jane was only 14 at the time of her mother's death. Elspet's sister Jane Turner, married John Weir and **Alexander pictured left** was their son. Jane Forsyth therefore married her first cousin Alexander Weir in 1867. My father told us that he knew his grandparents were cousins.

The story Dad told us was that his brother Jimmy had come home from school one day and asked their grandmother Jane, who was visiting at the time, if it was true that the children of cousins were *"feels"* (fools). My great grandmother's quick response was, *"Was your father a feel?"* Nothing more was said.

James Willcox, son of my cousin Ian Willcox, has also been researching the Weir family and sent me the marriage certificate. At the foot of the marriage certificate under Jane's name it states "cousins German" which was the term used to record that the couple were first cousins. They were living together at the time of their marriage.

# Chapter 5 Part 1 - My Father's Story

**Marriage Certificate of Alexander and Jane Forsyth Weir**

Alexander had five brothers and two sisters. He died in 1908 and in his will, he left the farm of Clerkseat to his youngest son Robert, who was unmarried and in poor health. Robert was not expected to live a long life and on his death the farm was to be sold and the proceeds divided between the surviving sons including my grandfather Alexander Weir. When Jane had become too old and infirm herself to provide the care which Robert, who was wheelchair bound, required, the family employed a nurse to look after him.

My father told us that, after an extremely short relationship, his Uncle Robert married the nurse when he was too ill to know what was happening, Dad had told me this story several times, so it was interesting to have it confirmed, at least date wise by Ancestry.co.uk. Robert married the nurse on 3rd December 1930. He died the following August, aged 52. My father told us that Robert signed over the farm and all its assets to the nurse on his deathbed. My father believed his uncle was coerced into doing this by the nurse. Grandpa Weir and his brother John's relatives were furious as they believed they had been cheated out of their rightful inheritance by the nurse. Dad used to drive past the farm and never failed to mention the story of his lost inheritance. He was quite bitter about it.

# From Barbados to Banffshire

**My grandfather, also Alexander Weir, was born on 17th June 1874 in Marnoch, Banffshire.**

Grandpa Weir was a well-known and successful sheep farmer in the Northeast of Scotland, He married my grandmother Helen Webster in 1900.

I always thought he looked quite stern in the photograph on the left. It is a copy of a life-size photograph in a large ornate frame. Along with an equally large even more imposing portrait of his father, also Alexander Weir (see previous paragraph), it used to look down at us from a wall in my grandmother's house.

After my grandmother died in 1962, the portraits were moved to our own house in Rothiemay, so I was used to seeing them while growing up. When my father sold our Crossroads Farm, they migrated to the dining room of Upper Crichie farmhouse, the home of my sister Gladys and her husband, Peter. I am informed by Gladys that they have been relocated to a back bedroom after spooking the family by both falling off the wall in the dining room. Great grandfather came off worst as his frame was broken. Gladys has managed to take the photograph of the abandoned portrait which is seen in the previous paragraph.

Although I thought Grandpa Weir looked as if he disapproved of the goings on in our house, my Dad's cousin Auntie Bess told me she remembered him to be a very gentle, approachable man who was well liked, and highly respected in the farming community.

James Willcox sent me the following information about Grandpa Alexander Weir's farming history:

*"The information from the valuations rolls shows that he was always a tenant farmer. I believe he started at Shank of Barry before*

# Chapter 5 Part 1 - My Father's Story

*moving onto Newtack (Owned by Duke of Fife), then Airdiecow (Owned by Earl of Seafield) and finally to Cornhill before buying the Crown Hotel. It appears that each farm is slightly bigger and therefore demonstrates a sense of growing prosperity. I found an interesting wee bit in a local paper from 1913 that writes*

*"On Christmas Eve, Mr Weir, farmer at Ardiecow, Deskford set in motion a fine new threshing mill made by Barclay, Ross and Tough, Aberdeen. With the help of some friends and neighbours, a thresh took place. The mill will be of great advantage, for with Ardiecow being at a higher point, water wasn't always readily available. Following the thrash, a convivial evening was enjoyed by all." The spelling seems to be different, or the paper made a mistake.*

*My Grandmother (Peg Willcox) used to tell me about the farm and walking down to the school and Kirk in Deskford or "Deskert" as it is known locally while Alex and Jimmy went to Fordyce Academy. There were woods either side of the farm with one known as Alex's wood and the other as Jimmy's wood.*

*The Weirs seemed to occupy a number of farms around Grange and Grandma would often mention various members of the Weirs living at the likes of Clerkseat, Paithnick and Upper Skeith in addition to those mentioned above. It was a Margaret Weir Jamieson (Grandma's Aunty) that lived at Upper Skeith before moving to Broomlea in Cullen where later on Grandma was to live too."*

Around 1928 Grandpa's wife and daughters persuaded him to leave farming and buy the Crown Temperance Hotel in Banff. Two of his daughters, Nell and Frances, went to the School of Domestic Science in Aberdeen to learn the hotel trade. Grandpa realised he was outnumbered, especially as Grandma had also had enough of the farming life. Grandpa was not contented living at the hotel and complained to Dad that he was so bored he started smoking.

Grandpa resolved his situation by renting fields in Cairnhill Farm so that he could resume rearing his Border Leicester sheep which he loved doing. This was when he had his most successful run,

# From Barbados to Banffshire

winning a number of medals, and cups for champion sheep as well as ploughing. Most of them are dated from 1930 - 1935.

**Here is Grandpa
with one of his champion Border Leicester Sheep.**

**One of Grandpa's many medals
The enscription on the back reads:**

**M.F.C. 1930
A. Weir
Best P.B. Sheep**

Grandpa Weir died of a heart attack in 1941 at the age of 65. This was six years before our family arrived in Scotland. My father was disappointed that his father was unable to meet us all when he brought us to Scotland. I would have loved to have known him.

# Chapter 5 Part 1 - My Father's Story

**My Father Alexander Thomas Weir was born on 25th April 1901 in Newtack, Grange, Banffshire, Scotland.**

He was the oldest son of Alexander Weir and Helen Webster.

**My father as a small boy with his maternal grandmother Mary McEwan Webster**

Dad told us his earliest memory was a very sad one as he remembers his baby sister Mary dying and his parents weeping round her cot when he was a very young boy himself. He often told us of this tragedy and was clearly traumatised by it (see Chapter 8).

My father's childhood and his life as a young man was very different from my mother's experiences growing up. He grew up within the farming community of Banffshire (now known as East Aberdeenshire) in the Northeast of Scotland.

My sister Gladys remembers Dad saying that in the summer, he and his brother Jimmy had to walk the three miles to school, through fields, with bare feet. They wore what was known as "tackety boots" in the winter. He told Gladys this when he had to take her to buy new school shoes. Dad did like to exaggerate the hard life he said he had, especially when he was having to spend money. Lunch was a bowl of soup from a friend of his mother who lived near the school.

Dad was a clever scholar and his school leaving certificate confirms this. He left school when he was 14 years old to undertake farm work at a neighbouring farm, while also helping his own father in his "spare time". His mother told me he used to say he wanted to be a minister. I couldn't quite imagine him in a pulpit, somehow. The subjects my father studied at Deskford School were listed on his school leaver's certificate dated 19th August 1915 as follows:

# From Barbados to Banffshire

*English - VG, Arithmetic - G, Handwriting - VG, Laws of Health - VG, Nature Study - Excellent, The Empire and its Growth - Excellent. Special subjects were Geometry - Excellent, Woodwork - VG.*

He had very artistic handwriting, but I don't remember him doing much woodwork. Mum said he did not have the patience.

Gladys remembers a conversation she had with our Grandma Weir when she told Gladys that she was very disappointed that Dad left school to work on a farm. Grandma had told him he would be like "*a square peg in a round hole*" as he was too intelligent to work on a farm. After leaving Deskford school he did attend Fordyce Academy for further education in evening classes and his report card from there said he was an excellent student. Gladys has a book Dad received as first prize when he was in primary school entitled "Two to One, The Tale of a Holiday" by Florence Coombe (1907 edition). Her son Peter has it now and reads it to his own children.

Not long after his brother Jimmy had been home on leave from Malaysia, my father received a letter from his cousin Mary Smith, formerly of Tarmore, Keith, inviting him to join her and her husband in Demerara, British Guiana, and become an overseer on a sugar plantation. However, Dad felt responsible for helping his father, so continued to work on the farm for a while. He did give it some thought, and then, after much deliberation, feeling that it was too good an opportunity to miss, he decided he did want to go. He travelled to Liverpool and boarded a ship for British Guiana. The year was 1927 and at the age of 26 he emigrated to that country, which was the only British colony on the South American continent.

Dad was employed as an overseer by a company called Booker Brothers, now known as Guysuco. He was eventually promoted to become the manager of the sugar plantation in Demerara, called Dekinderen, in 1939.

# Chapter 5 Part 1 - My Father's Story

**Dad hunting for Caiman on the Demerara River. Dad is the man on the right in the photo.**

Dad was befriended and made welcome by several Scottish people already in Demerara.

He enjoyed his bachelor life in British Guiana. Apart from his hunting pursuits he also enjoyed playing tennis and riding the mules on the plantation.

The new life in Demerara was not without its stresses. There was still a degree of resentment experienced by the white managers from the canecutters who were often direct descendants of the enslaved. It was understandable considering they might still remember their grandparents, or great grandparents, telling of how enslaved persons were deprived of their rights as human beings. Dad told us a story of a previous estate manager who was riding alongside a row of trees on the plantation, when a cane worker, hiding up a tree, attacked the manager with a cutlass, cutting off his hand. The manager had raised his hand to protect himself when he realised he was in danger. Dad admitted that because of this warning, and because of the poisonous snakes which came into the house, he felt the need to sleep with a gun under his pillow for the protection of himself and his family.

Dad was allowed home leave every two years. When he arrived home on his first leave from British Guiana, in 1929, Dad had been disappointed to discover the farm had been given up so soon. He felt guilty for having left his father at that time. When he came home again in 1932, Dad was pleased that his father had been able to resume his sheep farming and was happier within himself. He had even bought what was believed to be the first car to be seen in Banff. Dad couldn't wait to have a shot of it. Without having any

# From Barbados to Banffshire

lessons or insurance, he invited his sisters to come for a spin in the car. Dad managed to crash the car and his sister Nell was knocked unconscious. Nell recovered but Dad's reputation for being the dependable, if a bit boring, brother took a hit.

**Here is Dad with his sisters Nell and Frances with Cousin Agnes just before crashing his father's new car when home on leave in Banff in 1932.**

Approximately eight years after arriving in British Guiana, my father met and fell in love with my mother, Constance Margot Turpin (see Chapter 4 Part 1 for her life story). They were married on 29th April 1940. There was a considerable age difference as Dad was seventeen years her senior. Unfortunately, he did not have a strong constitution and the heat and poor water quality played havoc with his health. He contracted dysentery and had great difficulty fighting off the infection which this caused. He was quite ill just after getting married in 1940 and lost a lot of weight. The dysentery worsened over the years as he was not given the correct treatment. It was misdiagnosed as diarrhoea in British Guiana. In 1946, after the war had ended, Dad made plans to take his long overdue home leave. He was looking forward to introducing his wife and children to his mother and sisters. His Company doctor recommended that he make an appointment to see a Harley Street Specialist in London because of his ill health. When Dad returned to Scotland in 1947, the specialist diagnosed the illness as Colitis. This deteriorated further to become ulcerative colitis. Dad suffered intermittent bouts

124

of bad health, throughout his life in Guyana, and subsequently in Scotland.

Dad was obviously highly thought of by his employers as they told him that on his return from his holiday to Scotland, he was to be offered a directorship in the company. When he did not return, they paid him a pension and continued to pay my mother a small pension until she died in 2008.

## Back home to Scotland

As detailed in my mother's story, in early 1947, we left British Guiana and travelled in a troop ship back to England, staying briefly in a snowy London before travelling to Banffshire to visit Dad's mother and sisters.

Soon after our arrival Dad made the train journey back down to London to see the specialist. The news from the medical check-up was not good and Dad was warned not to return to Demerara as the climate was exacerbating his condition.

This was a huge blow, especially for my mother who had to send a telegram to her parents and tell them to "Sell everything. We are not coming back". It was a very different life that Dad came back to in Scotland compared to the colonial lifestyle he had enjoyed.

After approximately six months living in Banff with his mother and then about 18 months in a cottage in the village of Cuminestown, Dad bought a farm one mile from the village of Rothiemay. This was in 1949.

It took my parents, especially my mother a period of time to adjust to the completely different climate and lifestyle. However, Dad soon settled into his life as a Scottish farmer and got on well with the local farmers. His close neighbour, Willie Wilson, who was married to Dad's cousin Alice Webster used to visit regularly and we were quite amused listening to his very broad Doric accent. Doric is the popular name for the Northeast Scots language. It was like a foreign language to us at first. Dad was bilingual in that he could switch

# From Barbados to Banffshire

from broad Doric to perfect English in a heartbeat. If a local farmer phoned the house, we could tell it wasn't the minister or the headmaster by Dad's responses.

Dad was much in demand for giving talks throughout the community on his life in Demerara. I remember him showing me a beautifully written essay, which he used to speak from called "Twenty Years in British Guiana". I am disappointed that I have been unable to find this document as it would have given some very good insights into his life there. He was confident and humorous, quite a change from when as a young man he felt he lacked the confidence of his brother Jimmy.

Dad was always very outspoken. Anyone asking his opinion was told exactly what he thought. The local minister at the time, Reverend Michael Dickie, knew that if he asked my father for his opinion on his sermons, he would get the truth. I can remember Dad telling him as we left the church after the service one morning something like, "*Well Mr Dickie, I'm afraid that sermon had me thinking of all the work I'd have been better doing out in the fields on such a fine day*". I cringed with embarrassment. Mr Dickie told me that Dad also gave him encouragement saying he had given him "food for thought", and he valued Dad's opinions. Apart from becoming a full-time farmer of 88 acres mixed farming, Dad became the President of the Young Farmers Club. He was an elder at the local church in Rothiemay as well as father to us five "quines". One of his quips to farmers who commented that he must be disappointed he had no sons, would be to say "*Aye that's right. The only thing I ever had a guid crop o' was a bunch o' useless quines*", when he knew perfectly well I was within earshot. He loved to tease.

## Farm Girls?

When Margaret and I were twelve and ten years old respectively, Dad decided to give us a chance to rear our own cocks for the market. He bought us about 50 or so cock chicks or capons and we had to get up early in the morning before going to school to feed them. We had to "fatten them up for the market". He bought the food, but we knew we had to pay him back when the cocks were

126

# Chapter 5 Part 1 - My Father's Story

sold. I was sure we would be rich when we sold them and planned to buy lots of toys with the money. However, when the cocks were sold, we had a reality check when we discovered how little money was left over after the purchase price of the chicks, their food and antibiotics were paid for. We were allowed to buy ourselves new raincoats with our profits. Mine was royal blue. I don't remember buying any toys and I never became a businesswoman, neither did Margaret. Gladys and Betty were also given the opportunity to make some money rearing cock chicks. However, they were more successful than Margaret and me because Gladys can remember an enjoyable trip to Huntly on the bus when she and Betty were able to spend their profits. Lucky them.

**Father of Teenage Girls**

When we reached our teenage years and started going to the local dances, Dad was embarrassingly protective of us at first. As President of the Young farmers Club, he was often required to be at the door of the Grange Hall taking the entrance money. He was a very good dancer and liked to show off his prowess on the dance floor by taking us girls up to dance in turn. When he got tired, having been out working in the fields from sunrise, Dad would ask some of the local lads to dance with us. Not one had ventured forth to ask the remaining wallflowers to dance while he was dancing with any of us. It was excruciatingly cringeworthy when he would cross the floor to the line of stationary young men, some still smelling of the cows they had been working with, and wearing their working boots, and plead, "*Will nane o' you loons come and dance wi' my quines.*" Oh, how we wished for the floor to open and swallow us. We were rather unflatteringly referred to as, "*The Quine Weirs*" as they muttered to each other, "*You go. No you go*".

Dad was very security conscious and made no secret of the fact that he had a shotgun (known in farming circles as a "double barreller"). A boy who wanted to "see me home" from a dance told me that the word around the neighbourhood was that "*Auld Weir stood at the upstairs window with his gun*", in wait for any boy who might be taking any of us home. I told him this was not true and I'm

127

# From Barbados to Banffshire

not sure if he was making excuses not to see me home or if he really believed that. He did see me home but did not hang about.

I do recall a rather scary incident when I was asleep in the only downstairs bedroom: we called it "the maid's room". I heard a noise outside and, seeing a light on in a shed, I alerted my father that we might have an intruder. He leapt out of bed and clattered down the stairs with his boots on shouting "*Whaur's my double bareller?*" and proceeded to exit the backdoor ready for action. I was terrified that some unfortunate would-be thief might meet his maker at my father's hand. Thankfully, there was no one there and he decided a farm hand must have left the light on. I did confront him about this and asked if he would have used his gun on the intruder. His reply was, "*Not if he was running away, but if he was coming towards me I might.*" I was about 16 years old at the time and was not sure if he was joking.

When I was about 17 and had met my future husband, Norman, I was allowed to go to dances with him. Dad was always concerned that I was home by midnight as he did not think I should be "*oot galavantin' on a Sunday morning, and me an elder o' the kirk.*" If I did not make it home before midnight, I can still see and hear him clattering down the stairs in his tackety boots, wearing his thick woollen "long john combination" night attire, hair standing on end, no teeth, and a face like thunder. My excuses were ignored, even if I had a good one.

On one memorable night we had been at a barn dance in the middle of nowhere when a strong wind buried our car in cut grass while it was parked in the field outside the venue. Dad looked at me suspiciously when I stuttered out the story. He then shouted his mantra about being an elder o' the kirk. When he saw I had company he turned and went back up the stairs. Norman, looking sheepish, made a hasty retreat. I like to believe that Dad had been worried about me and was relieved I was home safe. My sisters can remember these occasions vividly.

# Chapter 5 Part 1 - My Father's Story

## Farmer or Gardener?

Dad was a very tidy person and, as well as always dressing impeccably when he was going out, he liked to have the garden looking nice. The farmhouse was on the crossroads between the road from Rothiemay to Keith and the road from Banff to Huntly, so the garden was in full view of passing traffic. Hence our address was Crossroads Farm, Rothiemay. To celebrate the Queen's Coronation in 1953, Dad planted out our garden very patriotically in flowering plants of red, white, and blue. Dad's farming friends used to tell him they couldn't understand how he got time to do gardening as they didn't bother and needed to spend all their time farming.

We all had to help Dad with harvesting. I can remember when driving the tractor, I had to stand on the brakes because my legs were too short to reach the pedals. Margaret would sit on the Clydesdale horse called Bloom which pulled a cart with me on top of it catching the sheafs of corn. Her job was to guide the horse and cart between the stooks. I had to arrange the sheafs on the cart: not my favourite job. We fed the hens, collected eggs, and mucked out their henhouses. If I wanted to go to a dance in the Grange Hall, I had to earn the entrance money of 3 shillings by cleaning out a henhouse. I hardly had time to have a bath before going and on at least one occasion can remember having to pick bits of straw out of my hair when I saw myself in the mirror in the cloakroom.

**Dad putting the finishing touches to the corn ricks.**

# From Barbados to Banffshire

## Avril's Memories of Dad

Avril is eight years younger than I am, so her memories of Dad are somewhat different to mine. Here are a couple of her stories. She was affectionately referred to by Dad as "*The Bairn*".

*"Dad was a staunch Conservative and used to support our MP at the time. Wilfred Harold Kerton Baker was the Member of Parliament for Banffshire from 1964 to 1974, when he lost his seat in the February election of that year to Hamish Watt of the Scottish National Party. His wife came to the house quite often and on one memorable occasion when she called to deliver leaflets for Dad to distribute, was chased down the garden path by our goat Mitzi, who had been tethered in the back garden but got loose, obviously a sensible animal that had no truck with Tories! I don't think Mrs Baker had ever moved so fast.*

*One morning when I was very young Dad took me to visit Mrs Kidd who lived in the neighbouring croft house, and I remember being fascinated by the box bed at the side of the fireplace. I used to enjoy going there as she always gave me milk and chocolate biscuits. On this occasion, however, I was aware that she did not seem like herself. It turned out her husband had hanged himself in the barn a couple of days beforehand and I remember her telling Dad how she had gone to look for him and found him hanging. Dad had been there to give his condolences and had taken me with him!!"*

Avril was only three years old, so Dad probably thought she was not aware of what they were talking about. However, she remembers the occasion vividly. In those days Child Psychology was quite unheard of especially amongst the farming community. The family friend, Roy Skinner, used to recite the following poem when he joined us for family dinners. "*Child Psychology? Haud yer tongue, there was nae sic thing when I was young*".

# Chapter 5 Part 1 - My Father's Story

## Retirement

Dad's health continued to cause concern for as long as I can remember. None of us were considered to be capable of taking over the farm, ("*just useless quines!*") so the farm was sold in 1966. Dad felt he had no option as he was just not well enough to carry on. The family moved to a terraced house in St Catherine Street, Banff. This suited my teenage sisters, who enjoyed the freedom of living in the town, but Dad did not enjoy living in Banff. He would get very irritated at seeing random members of the public walking past the living room window as the house was on the street with no front garden.

Mum told us that she felt he had been bullied into buying the house by his three sisters, who were the only people I knew who seemed to get away with telling him what to do. After a few years of fuming about people invading his space, he bought a cottage in the country some three miles from Banff. It had once been a toll house, so it was quite a quaint hexagonal shape. He enjoyed the large garden there. After it was sold, it was demolished to make way for a modern house.

Dad's health did not improve, and after having enjoyed only three years living in the countryside again, he had to go to hospital for a colostomy operation. He had always resisted this operation as he knew he would hate living with the inconvenience. When Margaret and I visited him in hospital in the February before he died in 1971, his last words to us as we left his bedside were, "*I'm going out of here in a box*". By the time Margaret and I arrived back to see him the second time, he was unconscious. Our father died soon after in Aberdeen Royal Infirmary on 26th March in 1971. He is buried in Banff Cemetery with his parents and other family members. I remember feeling that the cornerstone of our lives had gone. Although we argued about lots of things, I loved and respected him and do know that as a father he did his best to keep us safe.

# From Barbados to Banffshire

**The Weir Family Portrait.**

**Back row**: Jimmy, Peg, Alec (Dad)
**Front row**: Grandma, Frances, Bunty, Nell, Grandpa

**Dad's siblings are listed as follows:**

Mary Jane Forsyth Jan 1903-July 1903
William **James** Dec 1905-1939.
Margaret **(Peg)** 1906-2001.
Helen McConachie **(Nell)** -1908-1972.
**Frances** Forbes 1910 -1978.
Alice **(Bunty)** 1913-1945.

# Chapter 5 Part 2 - Paternal Aunts and Uncle

## William James Weir was born on 21st January 1905

James (known as Jimmy) my father's only brother was four years younger. I have very little information on Jimmy as a child other than that he had a sunny nature and was very popular, always laughing and joking.

There was a serious downturn in the fortunes of farming in the period just after the First World War in the early 1920's. Uncle Jimmy left the farming life first and went to Malaysia or Malay States as it was known then, to seek his fortune on the rubber plantations.

**Uncle Jimmy Relaxing in Malaysia**
Dad often told us the story of Jimmy arriving home on leave, around 1926, to be "welcomed with open arms." A celebratory roast dinner was prepared, and all the family were invited. Dad was aggrieved, as he felt that Jimmy had left him and their father to do all the work on the farm.

Dad told us he did not have time to partake in the celebration as there was too much to do out in the fields. Listening to the story did remind me of the biblical prodigal son and the fatted calf. However, there is nothing in the family history to suggest that Jimmy squandered his father's money. Indeed, he appears to have done quite well and was full of exciting stories to enthral the family with.... well, not all the family.

Dad told us that Jimmy was a popular charismatic fellow with the "gift of the gab", unlike himself. Dad claimed that, as a young man, he was himself more introverted and uncomfortable socially.

Uncle Jimmy sadly died at the youthful age of 34 in 1939 from Malaria complications. He died in hospital only days before the Japanese soldiers entered Malaysia and, with bayonets, killed the remaining patients as they lay in their beds. The family had some comfort from knowing Jimmy had died before the Japanese soldiers came. The family were told that he too would have met this terrible fate had he been still alive at the time of the invasion. At the time of his death, he was engaged to an Australian nurse, and he had been looking forward to getting married after the war.

**Margaret Weir / Willcox (Auntie Peg) was born on 25th August 1906 in Grange, Banffshire**

Auntie Peg was a very gracious lady who was the oldest of the four Weir sisters. They were all strong intelligent women, very independent and capable in their chosen professions. Peg was a good-looking woman, every inch a lady, who could be slightly intimidating. I remember having to be on my best behaviour when in her company as I was growing up.

Aunty Peg trained as a nurse at the Victoria Infirmary in Glasgow in the 20s. Around 1933 or 34 she joined Princess Mary's Royal Air Force Nursing Service at Halton Hospital in Runcorn. She then travelled with the RAF to Iraq working as a nurse. During her time in Iraq, she met Uncle Hilton who was a doctor in the RAF. They fell in love, got engaged, then came home to be married in the Hill O'Doune church in MacDuff on 4th August 1937.

Hilton Willcox was born in New Zealand. He was a Captain Scott type of adventurer, travelling on Antarctica expeditions. He has written about his adventures in his book called "Beneath a Wandering Star". He has also authored an interesting book about his travels as a Group Captain Doctor in the RAF, as well as his family life. It is entitled "Travels by Command" and is as yet unpublished. I have read some of it and his worldwide travel experiences make absorbing reading.

Uncle Hilton presented to us children with a stern demeanour. He was a handsome man with an air of authority. I got the impression that my best behaviour was necessary around him as well as his wife. I do think that had I been able to pluck up the courage to ask him to talk about his travels, I would have found him very interesting to listen to.

**Auntie Peg and Uncle Hilton had three children who are pictured below.**

**Hylton, Margaret and Ian**

Their first son, Hylton, was born on the 7th July 1938. He was called up for national service when he was 18 years old and at the end of his 2 years decided to train as a pilot officer in the Royal Air Force. He learned to fly on Jet Provost Aircraft at RAF Oakington, near Cambridge.

The following information is quoted from his father's book, "Travels by Command":

*"He loved flying. Of the 4 cups available to trainee pilots, he won 3 and came second in the 4th subject (ground training). He was appointed course leader; and the future beckoned to him with outstretched wings, assuring him of a brilliant career in the modern air force. At the end of his course in Oakington, his proud parents were going there to attend the Wings parade, at which his Pilot's wings would be pinned on his tunic, and he would be presented with the three cups he had won. The evening before his Wings parade, he was killed in a road accident near his base. The date was September 21,1959. He was 21."*

# From Barbados to Banffshire

The day the news of this tragedy came through to us by phone in Rothiemay is a vivid memory for me. Grandma was particularly saddened by this, saying, "It should have been me who died." Our whole family was in shock. His father goes on to describe his son Hylton as "*A happy boy, with a joyous personality*" and "*In a moment, on a road made slippery by the first rains after a dry summer, streaming on to a bending Cambridgeshire Road, and its mud and oil, he was gone*".

We were told that Hylton, on noting that the road was dangerously slippery, had stopped his car to get out and warn his friends, who were travelling behind him, to be careful. In a dreadful irony, our caring young cousin was to lose his own life not much further along the road.

Ian was born in 1940 on the day of my parents' wedding, 29th April. I have been happy to renew our acquaintance now that we are both retired. He sent me the following information:

"*Our travels started in May 1949 when we left for Southern Rhodesia for 3 years where my father worked in Bulawayo, and we all lived on a small farm about 25 miles outside. We all had a great time in Rhodesia except my mother was not too keen on being left in the middle of the bush with only the African servants for company! When we returned in 1952, we stayed with Grandma Weir for several months while my father sorted out a house in London. We children went to Banff Academy for the rest of the summer term. So, 3 years in London and then 3 years in south Devon followed by 3 years in Gloucestershire near Cheltenham. We boys went off to Strathallan for the rest of our schooling. I later went on to Nottingham University and read mechanical engineering but was always associated with the steel industry both here and overseas. It was in 1961 that my parents went off to Singapore, which was the start of their far eastern travels, living in Hong Kong for several years before retiring to Cullen*".

Ian has 2 children from his first marriage to Virginia. They are Lucy and James. Lucy's children are Izaak and Nancy. James has 3 grownup children. They are Jessica who is sadly disabled due to

# Chapter 5 Part 2 - Paternal Aunts and Uncle

cerebral palsy, Lewis and Ciaran. James lectures in social care in Glasgow. He has been helping me with some of the Weir family history. Ian is now retired and lives in Surrey with his second wife Lucia, who is from Brazil. Lucia has a vibrant outgoing, friendly personality. They have a daughter Joanna who has 2 children, Callum (7) and Emilia. (5).

Margaret was born in 1942, and was 9 months older than I am. I remember her growing up as a beautiful, talented young girl. Sadly, I have had only minimal contact with her since we grew up and settled in opposite parts of the UK. I was sad when I learned that she developed Parkinson's Disease some 20 years ago. She died in January 2022. Parkinson's is a progressive disease which rendered her severely disabled, and she was wheelchair bound by the time she died. Margaret remained very aware and able to communicate with her close family and carers. Her husband Richard Gowring, who had been her main carer, and her "rock" sadly died in December 2019 following a stroke and developing dementia. This left them with no option but to move into a care home.

Richard Gowring was descended from the Scottish bard, Robert Burns and Jean Armour, his long-suffering wife. Richard had been the keeper of the Burns Heritage Archives, but since his illness and death, his daughters Sheena and Fiona are now undertaking this role. I only met him a few times. Richard is described in an obituary, which has been put online by the Burns Heritage society. Here is an excerpt:

*"His kindness, unerring devotion to caring for his wife with Parkinson's for over 20 years and his cracking sense of humour will be missed by all."* I wish I had known him better.

Margaret and Richard are survived by two daughters and four grandchildren. The oldest, Sheena (Whitehouse), has 2 children, Thomas and Hannah. They live near Oxford. Fiona (Brent) has 2 daughters, Charlotte, and Emily. They live near Portsmouth. I have not met them, but we are able to keep in touch on Facebook.

# From Barbados to Banffshire

Auntie Peg and Uncle Hilton retired to Cullen, Banffshire to a villa called "Broomlea" which had belonged to her Auntie Maggie, one of her father's sisters. Uncle Hilton predeceased her in 1987 and she moved to Lythe Nursing Home, Cullen, where she died on 8th July 2001, aged 95. When visiting her in the Nursing home I was made aware by the staff that she insisted on always being addressed as "Mrs Willcox", never her first name.

## Helen McConachie Weir / Miller (Nell) was born in Banffshire in 1908

Auntie Nell was also an independent, intelligent woman like her sisters and her mother. She and Uncle Bob Miller were a significant influence on the lives of my parents and our family. I had regular contact with her while growing up, but not so much later. She trained at the Aberdeen School of Domestic Science to become a hotelier which was her occupation all her life. Auntie Nell married Uncle Bob on 12th December 1945. They had bought the Crown Hotel Banff from her mother when she retired some years earlier.

We visited the hotel often while growing up. My aunt was always busy. She was a hands-on hotelier. Sometimes when we were in Banff on a school outing, we would pop in past the hotel to see her. My sisters and I would be ushered into the hotel living room just to look at each other as she would say "*A hinna time*" (I haven't). On other occasions, when we were older, we would be taken into the large hotel kitchen and given a job drying dishes.

Auntie Nell and Uncle Bob kindly helped my parents by taking me, a very active outspoken 4-year-old, to stay with them at the hotel after my sister Betty was born. This was intended to relieve the childcare tasks in Grandma's house. My Aunt and Uncle had been disappointed not to have children and would have liked to have me remain with them. However, I was not keen on this and preferred to go back to living with my parents and sisters. This story is covered in more detail in my own life story.

Auntie Nell did not enjoy a good relationship with her mother: a personality clash of two strong personalities, I think. She told my

# Chapter 5 Part 2 - Paternal Aunts and Uncle

mother that her mother, while singing the praises of her sisters, Peg (for her beauty), and Frances (for her intelligence), would tell Nell she was only good for scrubbing floors. I have to say that of the three sisters I did find Nell the most likeable for all her apparent lack of social graces and tact.

My aunt and uncle did succeed in adopting a baby boy from Glasgow in 1952. They had him christened "Wallace" which was Uncle Bob's middle name. I remember seeing photos of Wallace wearing the christening robe my father wore for his own baptism in 1901.

I am not sure how much information my aunt and uncle had been given about his parents but unfortunately they had not been advised as to how their son should be told about his origins. Wallace only found out he was adopted from his fellow school pupils and his adoptive parents were quite hurt when he demanded to know more. Nell told my mother that she told Wallace that his mother need be of no interest to him and that he should think of her as dead to him. I believe he did go looking for her but I do not think he found her. This caused a rift between them and the relationship became strained. There was no such thing as adoption support in those days and Auntie Nell would have been acting purely on instinct.

Adoption in the Northeast of Scotland was usually done within families as I describe in my own life story. I feel sorry for my aunt and uncle who would have had no professional help or advice as to how to handle the delicate subject of helping their son to understand his background. I suspect that this personal knowledge of unsupported adoption contributed to my subsequent desire as a social worker to take a special interest in adoption.

We had quite a lot of contact with Wallace growing up; he was well treated and very indulged materially. He visited us with his parents at the farm from time to time but was not interested in farming. My father used to say he was very spoiled and they did not get on.

Avril was of similar age to Wallace so knew him better than I did but they were not close. Auntie Frances was very fond of Wallace and

# From Barbados to Banffshire

was quite upset when he disappeared from the family. We think he may have settled in the USA as the last unconfirmed news any of us had of him was that he was working as an electrician in California for Rod Stewart.

Auntie Nell became ill with cancer of the uterus and died in Banff Hospital on 8th January 1972 at the age of 64. Uncle Bob died in 1978, also in Banff.

We lost touch with Wallace after his mother died and we have no idea where he is or whether he is even still alive. This is quite sad.

**Frances Forbes Weir was born in Banffshire, in 1910**

Frances was an intelligent, attractive woman oozing self-confidence but with an acerbic side to her nature. She also knew how to dress well. Auntie Frances, like her mother, brother and sisters, was also very outspoken. Like her older sister Nell, she went to train at the School of Domestic Science in Aberdeen known as "The Doh School". When their parents bought the Crown Temperance Hotel in Banff, she and Auntie Nell both worked there helping their mother in the hotel. During the war, Frances was employed at the Food Office in Banff.

Frances was then employed for a number of years as the manageress of the Aberfeldy Hotel. She enjoyed living in Aberfeldy and named her retirement bungalow after the town.

Auntie Frances bought the Grant Arms Hotel at Cullen in the 1950s. I remember visiting there with my father and my sisters. We were not exactly welcomed with open arms. She used to complain loudly about having to fork out her hard-earned cash in tax to pay for family allowance when she had no children herself. It made her "see red". Auntie Frances never married but did get engaged at least twice. "*She was far too independent for any man*", my Dad used to say. She enjoyed being the hostess at the Grant Arms and Gladys remembers Frances entertaining the hotel guests in the bar, singing and playing the piano. Gladys was employed as an assistant at the hotel during her summer holidays. It was very hard work and she

# Chapter 5 Part 2 - Paternal Aunts and Uncle

was often expected to work from dawn to dusk without a break. Her accommodation was a caravan in the grounds. Being the owner's niece did not do her any favours. She found her aunt to be quite a formidable task mistress. I don't think any of us were particularly close to Auntie Frances, but she did give us nice presents at Christmas. Gladys and I were pleasantly surprised when she left us £100 each in her will. We learned that this was because we were not in employment at the time, unlike Margaret, Betty and Avril.

Frances developed brain cancer and died on 31st December 1978. I remember visiting her in hospital and feeling very sorry for her.

**Alice (Bunty) Weir/Catto was born in Banffshire in 1913**

Bunty was an attractive girl with a sunny nature, my father used to say. Her mother told us she was musically talented. Bunty, Dad's youngest sister, married Doctor Forbes Catto and they lived in Glasgow. She very sadly died in childbirth in 1945, while giving birth to twins. She was 32 years old. Cause of death was eclampsia and toxaemia. The twins only lived for a few hours. This was a sad loss for my grandmother, my father and his sisters. As far as I am aware, they did not have any ongoing contact with her bereaved husband.

**Bunty's Wedding to Dr Catto with Frances as bridesmaid**

# From Barbados to Banffshire

**My paternal grandmother was born Helen Webster on 18th December 1877**

She was the fifth child of Thomas Webster and Mary McEwen. Thomas was born in New Deer in 1839. He died in Newtonmore, Glenbarry, Marnoch, Banffshire as the result of an accident. He is buried in New Deer churchyard, Aberdeenshire. His wife, Mary was born on 30th November 1844 in Boyndie, Banffshire. She died on 5th April 1927 at Westside, Forglen, Banffshire. She is buried in Marnoch Graveyard, Banffshire.

Grandma Helen Weir was born at "The Auds", her McEwen grandfather's farm at Boyndie, very close to Banff. She married my grandfather, Alexander Weir on 29th June 1900 and died on 17th April 1962 in Aberdeen Royal Infirmary.

Grandma was to be a huge influence on our family, and she was a real character, very forthright. She was a confident, capable woman representative of her time and the farming culture into which she was born. To understand what life experiences may have contributed to her stoic, strong persona, it is important to know that she, along with her siblings, experienced loss from a young age with the death of her father Thomas Webster. She was six years old. How does a small child in a large family process such a loss? Thomas died at the age of 46 when he fell off the back of a trailer which was being used to move furniture. Grandma must have learned resilience from her mother who was left to bring up a large family on very little money.

Further losses were to cause my grandmother sadness when her first daughter, Mary died, at the age of five months, her youngest son Jimmy at the age of 34, and then her youngest daughter Bunty at the age of 32. These tragedies must have affected her happiness, although it was not uncommon for parents to outlive their children in those times.

We knew where we stood with Grandma and that meant we should be "seen and not heard" as was the parenting mantra of that

# Chapter 6 Part 1 – Grandma Helen Weir

generation. Nevertheless, she was a very good support to my parents and helped a lot to inform my mother of the ways of the farming community in Northeast Scotland, and what was expected of a farmer's wife. She did have some sympathy for my mother's plight and understood how Mum, having been accustomed to a vastly different lifestyle in Guyana, would need all the help and advice she could get. Grandma was a valued source of information to us all. One of her more amusing traits was when she made it her business to educate my mother on the superstitions which were significant for her. Here are some examples:

1. Certain flowering plants were not to be taken into the house or they would bring bad luck (e.g. flowering currant). Mum thought the flowers were quite beautiful as the vivid pink of the blossom was one of the first signs of spring. It grows profusely throughout the Northeast of Scotland. I remember Mum expressing her disappointment when she was told by Grandma that she could not have a vase of those flowers in the house. She had picked a bunch to brighten the house for a visit from her mother-in-law.
2. Always leave a home you are visiting by the same door through which you entered. All sorts of misfortune would befall the family if you did not do this, such as bad health and loss of money. Mum took this very seriously and always insisted that guests followed this superstition. It has taken me quite a while to stop feeling obliged to keep doing this myself.
3. When arranging the bedroom furniture, the bed should face the door to allow an easy passage out of the room with a dead body.

These are only a few of many examples but are the ones which come immediately to my mind. My mother took these superstitions quite seriously and has passed them down through the generations. Even her grandchildren are aware of these superstitions today.

My mother never had to cook or clean in Demerara as she had a cook and servants to do all these tasks for the family. Grandma felt she needed to take on the task of teaching my mother to cook. We all reaped the benefits of Grandma's cooking lessons, even if at times we did not appreciate it. My least favourite was Scotch broth

# From Barbados to Banffshire

which always contained what I considered to be far too much barley and it was never soft enough for my palate. I can remember having to spend the afternoon looking at the uneaten soup congealing in my bowl, as we were not allowed to leave the dining table in Grandma's house until our food had all been eaten. If you simply could not eat it, then you got no pudding.

My younger sister Gladys was not yet two when we arrived at Grandma's house from Guyana. When my mother advised Grandma that Gladys was not able to eat some vegetables such as carrots if they had not been cooked long enough, my grandmother's immediate solution was to take the carrots off the plate, chew them herself and feed the softened food to my sister, oblivious of my mother's look of disbelief and horror as Gladys swallowed the food. We can be sure that this practice was common before mothers had access to food processors and commercially produced baby food. My mother would have preferred to cook the vegetables longer and used a fork but being a busy mother with ten children to feed, expediency would have been of the essence for Grandma's own mother Mary. Immediately after the war food was scarce. Provision of food was regulated through the use of ration books, so nothing was to be wasted. To access food, the ration books or coupons as well as money were essential.

Grandma used to be quite critical of modern inventions such as the radio. We girls would enjoy listening to pop music, which was ok so long as Grandma was not in the room. When she entered the room, you could be sure that she would make for the radio and switch it off, saying *"We'll shut it aff, that'll shut its moo* (mouth)". I can still see the offending radio sitting on a shelf in her sitting room.

Another disappointing episode, I recall vividly, was coming home from school to find Grandma stuffing my colouring books and magazines into the (thankfully as yet unlit) Rayburn cooker. She had come to visit and decided to check our bedrooms for tidiness. We had to face Grandma's obvious disapproval if we left these things lying about. *"A place for everything and everything in its*

# Chapter 6 Part 1 – Grandma Helen Weir

*place*" was another of her sayings. Very good advice of course. Grandma was very enthusiastic about tidiness.

One of Grandma's favourite hobbies was attending auctions. She would buy lots of stuff she did not intend to buy by putting up her hand to greet a familiar face without realising she was bidding for some item in the auction. We children were quite pleased to receive these items, although our parents were not so happy to have to find space for them. She bought us a windup gramophone on which we very much enjoyed playing records. Not long after that another gramophone appeared, a bit of an upgrade (unintended of course) on the previous one, so no harm done we thought. Dad was less amused as he would have to go to wherever these purchases had been made and collect Grandma and her larger items which she could not manage on the bus. We put these machines to good use as during the summer holidays we would put on concerts for any visiting relatives and our closest neighbours.

On one occasion I can remember Gladys dancing the Highland Fling to a Jimmy Shand record on the gramophone. The windup gramophone would only play as long as the person (often me) to whom the task of winding it up fell, paid attention. The music got slower and slower with Gladys looking like she was dancing "The Dying Swan" instead of the intended Highland Fling. Dad could stand it no longer crossing "the stage" to wind up the gramophone vigorously. I would protest saying that was my job but he would carry on regardless. Not a good look for the audience of which he was supposed to be a member.

Gladys recalls one of the times when, during the school summer holidays, she and Betty were visiting Grandma for a week in her home in Banff. They entered a talent competition during the gala. The song they were practising was "He's Got the Whole World in his Hands". Although Grandma said she did not like the song she went with them, taking one of her friends to the venue expecting to watch her granddaughters sing. However, they were to let her down badly as they could not sing for giggling.....Grandma was not amused.

# From Barbados to Banffshire

As Grandma aged, she did become quite forgetful and was increasingly confused. This did not stop her embarking on bus journeys to places she had not intended to visit and we could get quite worried about her ending up in some place where it was not so easy for Dad to find her. We felt quite sorry for her as Dad would lose patience and give her a telling off for causing him so much inconvenience and worry. As she became more infirm it was necessary for live-in help to be sought for her. These ladies rarely stayed very long as Grandma was not a very cooperative patient and often sacked the carer unceremoniously without informing her daughters or my father. She used to insist that they had stolen something but usually found the lost item long after the alleged thief had left her employment. Not long after a new carer had been duly installed, Grandma had the misfortune to fall out of bed and break her hip but the new carer did not hear her cries. Poor Grandma had the awful experience of lying on her bedroom floor in severe pain all night. She was eventually taken to hospital but died not long after that. She was 84. It was a very sad day for us all.

I have enjoyed remembering Grandma while writing this book. She never expressed any fondness verbally to any of us. She often compared us younger ones unfavourably to our oldest sister Margaret who was "*a good quiet quine*". She did not hug us or show us any affection. Gladys and I both adore our grandchildren and have no difficulty in expressing our love for them, either physically or verbally. We never knew our maternal grandmother, Connie, but I can't help feeling that had we known her she would have been very different. Was it the era or the area of Northeast Scotland? Grandma would have grown up experiencing very few expressions of endearment herself, either physically or verbally from anyone. Fortunately, she somehow managed to impart enough feeling towards us, for us to remember her with fondness as well as respect.

# Chapter 6 Part 2 – The Webster Family

My cousin Jean Martin takes up the story now. Her information is in italics.

**Back Row; John, Annie, William, Jean, Tom, Maggie and Alex**
**Front Row; Helen, Lizzie, Mary McEwan (mother), Izzie and Mary**

*Helen was one of eleven children.*

*1) Isabella Bremner was the eldest. She was known as Izzie (17.06.64 – 06.06.26) and had been born to Mary out of wedlock, the father, William Bremner, signing the birth certificate. Isabella married Frank Forbes and they lived in Cullen.*

*2) Then came Elizabeth (b 17.04.1869) known as Lizzie. She lived with her mother at Muirden, Marnoch and died on 19th February 1919.*

# From Barbados to Banffshire

*3) The first boy John McEwen was born on 14th August 1871 in the Schoolhouse Boyndie, where Mary was the housekeeper. (Thomas Webster, the father, was working at Balgreen farm in the Parish of Gamrie at that time.). John married Annie Lumsden and farmed Greendykes, where they had three children - Elizabeth, who married Tom Davidson, a doctor in Aberdeen (daughter Aileen). Then came Thomas, who was later to farm Greendykes. He married Meta Morrison (Stella, Jennifer, Stanley, and Kenneth were their children.) The next child of John and Annie was Alice who married William Wilson (Bruckles).*

*John McEwen Webster died in Cornhill – the village, not the hospital - on 25th February 1954.*

**Guests at a Webster Wedding from left to right:
George Campbell, Bessie Webster, Alice Webster/Wilson,
Margot Turpin/Weir (Mum), Meta and Tom Webster,
Alec Weir (Dad), Willie Wilson**

# Chapter 6 Part 2 – The Webster Family

I remember these family members being visitors to our home. We used to visit at Greendykes when Tom and Meta lived there. We had great fun playing with the children and kept up the friendship with Jennifer for some time. Gladys has managed to renew their friendship in the last few months.

I have fond memories of Alice and Willie Wilson at Bruckles which was the neighbouring farm to ours at Crossroads. Willie was a very frequent visitor to the farm. We girls used to giggle at his very broad Doric accent when he was trying to make himself understood by my mother. If my father was not present, he had a habit of filling any silences in the conversation while waiting for Dad to appear with "*Tie, Tie*", (a Doric sigh?) whereupon I would have to leave the room in order not to lose control.

Willie visited my mother now and again at her home in Ellon after my father died. He was a very good friend to her. On one occasion when he turned up at her door with a suitcase, she became concerned that he may have mistaken their friendship for something else. What would the neighbours think! Her concern was soon abated when Willie revealed that the suitcase contained manure for her roses. We are still in touch with their son John who farms Bruckles now. He was in the same class as Betty at Rothiemay school.

*4) The second son was William who farmed Crannabog. He married Mary Anderson and they had four children – Mary Jane, John, William, and Amelia (Amy).*

*Mary Jane never married, and she worked as a housekeeper to a family in Aberdeen.*

*John, who was later to farm Crannabog, married Elizabeth Thomson and they had one daughter, Elizabeth, who taught English at Turriff Academy and married a David Christie (now divorced).*

# From Barbados to Banffshire

*William David (known as Davie) married Mary Jamieson and they had four children, Helen who married Allan Meldrum, Isobel who married William Duncan, William who married Frances Morrison and Andrew who married Mabel Dawson. Both William and Andrew are farmers while Helen and Isobel were both teachers. Davie farmed Little Whitefield and regularly entered his Border Leicester sheep at the Turriff Show, where he won lots of prizes. Peg Willcox, daughter of Helen and Alexander Weir, always maintained that the prize sheep were originally bred from a flock belonging to her father.*

*Amy was a nurse. She emigrated to Canada and lived near Vancouver. She was unmarried.*

I do remember Mary and Davy Webster and their family, especially Helen Meldrum who I had contact with a few years ago. Dad used to talk about Davy, and their shared interest in rearing Border Leicester sheep. Dad used to be disappointed when Davy's sheep won prizes while his never did. I used to think it might have had something to do with the fact that Davy was a lifelong farmer and did not go travelling across the Atlantic Ocean to grow sugarcane for 20 years and then come back to Scotland expecting to emulate his father's success. I decided not to share this view with him.

*5) Mary, the closest in age to Grandma Weir, married John Webster from an entirely different family of Websters. They came from Midmar and were millers at Auchintoul, also in Marnoch. They had three children - Mary who died of scarlet fever aged five, Agnes who married George Campbell and Elizabeth (Bess), who later married her widowed brother-in-law.*

*John Webster (Auchintoul) was an engineer in charge of the pattern making shop at the CPT, the Consolidated Pneumatic Tool Company in Fraserburgh.*

*The links between Mary and Grandma Weir were strong. Mary died in 1942 and 'Auntie Ellen' became an honorary grandmother to Jean, the daughter of Agnes and George Campbell. George, who ran a plasterer's business, had a yard in Banff, and a plasterer*

# Chapter 6 Part 2 – The Webster Family

*based there because of the work that was done in the area. He would travel from Fraserburgh to assess various jobs and so Auntie Ellen would get the odd trip around Banffshire, which she really enjoyed!*

Of all the Webster family cousins, my family's closest relationship was with Agnes, Bess and George Campbell as well as their daughter Jean with whom we are still in regular contact.

*6) Helen was the next child of Thomas Webster and Mary McEwen. She married Alexander Weir.*

*7) Anne came next. She married Robert Gordon and they farmed Gallowhill, also in the parish of Marnoch. They had nine children, the majority of whom were farmers or married to farmers. Their eldest son Robert, however, emigrated to Canada. There was Bella, (presumably Isabella), Thomas, Lizzie (Elizabeth) Dave, (David), Sandy (Alexander), Jessie, James, and William. If you landed up at Gallowhill about teatime on a Sunday, it was boiled eggs and the very best homemade oatcakes.*

*8) Margaret was the next daughter. She married David Geddes and they went to Durban in South Africa. They had three children, Ena, William, and David. The two boys died during World War II. Much earlier than that the family did return to Scotland for a visit.*

*9) Thomas, who married Annabella Elrick, was next in line. At one point he was stationmaster at Maud Railway Station, before farming at Strathellie, near Lonmay and latterly in a croft, Wardend, near St Combs. They had one daughter Margaret, who was unmarried.*

*10) Alexander was the last son of Thomas Webster and Mary McEwen. He was unmarried and worked in various farms around Banffshire.*

# From Barbados to Banffshire

*11) Jean was born after her father Thomas Webster died and she married James Chalmers. They farmed at Westside and retired to Cuminestown. Jean had one child before marriage, Mary Geddes whose father, so it is said, was the brother of David Geddes, married to Margaret Webster (South Africa.) It fell to Jean to look after her mother in her final days as she died at Westside in April 1927. The farm at Westside had a sway in the kitchen and a black kettle suspended from it even in the 1950s.*

*Mary Geddes was a lovely person who married Alexander Laurence. They farmed at Fattahead, Alvah and then at Hillhead of New Deer. Fattahead was where Jean Campbell, daughter of Agnes Webster, first learned to set up stooks! The Lawrences had six children: Alexander (Sandy), James, Peter, Ronnie, Ruby, and George. Ruby did marry a farmer George Paterson, but the brothers largely had careers away from farming.*

*The Chalmers children were Isabella (known as Bella) who married David Barr, Nellie, Peggy, Jemima who married Robert Scott late in life and Lizzie who was unmarried.*

Through my membership of Ancestry.co.uk I have been pleased to become acquainted with William Wallace, great grandson of Isabella and David Barr. William lives in Australia and we are friends on Facebook.

# Chapter 7 – My Life Story

## My Life Story

I was born in Georgetown, British Guiana, in August 1943 and was baptised by a Presbyterian minister, Reverend Birnie from Lossiemouth, who happened to be living in Demerara at the time. My father sought him out to baptise me. My grandfather Canon Turpin had baptised my sister Margaret, so Dad thought that it was only fair we were not all baptised in the Anglican church, especially since he was a staunch Presbyterian. I have continued to attend the Presbyterian church wherever I live, which at present is in Tarves, Aberdeenshire. The congregation is very welcoming and the minister, Reverend Dr Alison Swindells, now serves the whole area including Pitmedden, Methlick and Barthol chapel.

My early childhood was spent in a large estate house built on stilts within the grounds of Dekinderen Sugar Plantation where my father was the Manager. (See my mother's story for more about this). This was in Demerara, land of mud and the famous Demerara Sugar. People born there were known as "mudheads" because of the tendency for the Demerara River to burst its banks and flood the land, hence the need for the houses to be built on stilts.

## Earliest Childhood Memories

At Dekinderen, Margaret and I had a nanny each. Lilian was my nanny. and I still remember her face. She was a lovely brown skinned lady. There was a large garden where my sister Margaret and I would play in a sandpit under a palm tree. It seemed a long way from the house, but probably wasn't all that far. As I recount this story, I feel like I am that toddler of more than seventy years past. I recall the scene quite vividly. It had started to rain, and it was coming down in sheets, as tropical rain does. Margaret's nanny swept across the garden, and scooped up Margaret, leaving me bawling my head off, and feeling very frightened. After what seemed like ages, my mother came for me.

I later learned, when I was able to ask Mum about it, that it was due to a misunderstanding. It was Lilian's day off, and Mum had expected Margaret's nanny would have gone back for me.

# From Barbados to Banffshire

On another occasion which comes to mind I had wandered from the safety of our garden and found myself under the house. It was quite dark, and I could hear loud banging. It was scary. I saw some dark-skinned men who were hammering away and shouting loudly to each other. My father told me later that they were building a garage. I don't remember what happened next. My father told me later that I took a lot of looking after as I often went exploring without permission.

Another scary situation I can transpose myself back to in a flash was when I found myself in a large enclosure with large barking dogs in cages around the pen. I didn't realise they could not get out and was petrified. Mum told me later that they were guard dogs. Someone had left the gate to the enclosure open. To this day I'm not keen on big dogs.

**Me, Baby Gladys and Margaret**

When I was three years and seven months old, my parents, sisters and I crossed the Atlantic in what was a troop ship. This was in March 1947.

# Chapter 7 – My Life Story

My first memory of being on the ship was of looking through a round window (porthole) and seeing the sea splashing against the glass. My mother, my sisters, and I shared a small cabin, with bunk beds, and there was very little space to move around.

**This is me dressed as "Raggedy Ann"** at a fancy-dress competition on board ship. I got first prize which was a box of sweets.

**"I want some of that red stuff."**

The most outstanding memory I have of the journey was of being taken to a very large dining room to have my meals with my father, and a lot of men. They were soldiers returning to the UK after the war.

The passengers were segregated at mealtimes, according to gender. My sisters were given their meals with my mother. I went with my father quite happily and enjoyed the attention I got from the other diners. I don't remember feeling daunted by my dinner companions, but I do remember the echo of their loud voices, and the noisy clatter of plates. We sat down at a canteen type table and the food was served. It was the "red stuff" I saw being put on everyone's plate but mine which concerned me. They were all eating it and I thought it looked nice. I said to my father, "I would like some of that red stuff." He replied "No, you won't like it", then, to my great surprise, he put some on my plate. Dad was quite strict and not known for giving in to small children. It was the most disgusting stuff I had ever tasted. It was pickled beetroot, and I hate the taste to this day. A real "I told you so" moment for Dad, probably the first of many to come.

In a letter Leila Doobay to whom I refer in my mother's story, remembered my sister Margaret being a gentle child while I was "a

# From Barbados to Banffshire

busy body, full of mischief". This revelation was met with "No change there then" from my sisters. How dare they!

## Arrival in Banff

When we first arrived in England, on 17th March 1947, I have a hazy memory of arriving at a house where my father's sister, Auntie Peg, and her family lived. I do remember the whiteness, which I later learned was snow. It all seemed very strange to me after such a long sea voyage. My most vivid memories are of arriving in Scotland to live with my grandmother, Helen Weir, in her house in the town of Banff. It had a large back garden with a summer house in which we enjoyed playing.

**Here we are playing in Grandma's back garden.**

We were told to call her Grandma, and we knew her as Grandma Weir. She was quite stern, and I soon knew that she was a "no nonsense" kind of Grandma. There was a huge Grandfather clock halfway up the stairs. It kept me awake with a very loud tick tock. It chimed loudly throughout the night. It was creepy.

I was curious when a man turned up a few days after we arrived, asking to see us. "*Come along, children, the doctor has come to give you your injections*", I heard my mother say pleasantly. What was that? When I saw what was happening to Margaret, I sneaked out of the house and climbed up an apple tree in the back garden. I watched them from above as they searched for me down below and called my name. I did not come down off the apple tree until I thought the doctor had gone away. He returned later much to my

156

# Chapter 7 – My Life Story

unpleasant surprise. This time I tried hiding unsuccessfully under the chaise longue. My father held me down on the dining room table, screaming and kicking. I still hate injections but have learned not to kick and scream about it. Grandma was not pleased. This got us off on the wrong foot and I had the distinct impression that I was not her favourite. She called me "Precocious". I had no idea what that meant of course.

My sister Betty was born on 31st August 1947. I was proud to be allowed to rock her to sleep in Grandma's parlour when she was crying.

**Adoption? – Perhaps Not**

To put less pressure on my mother and Grandma, who were having to cope with four young children, including a new baby, I was taken to stay with my father's sister, Auntie Nell, and her husband, Uncle Bob. They owned The Crown Hotel, which was not far from Grandma's house in Banff. At first, I thought it was wonderful to have all the new toys bought for me, and to be made a fuss of by the hotel guests. However, sometimes I was left on my own with just the new toys as my aunt and uncle were usually busy working in the hotel. I got into trouble on one occasion for throwing the contents of a box of chalks one by one on the open fire. I experienced boredom for the first time in my short life, and missed the company of my sisters, Margaret and Gladys, even though we did squabble a lot. I adored my new baby sister Betty.

After having stayed at the hotel for a few months, I will always remember the day when I learned that Mum and Dad had bought a house in a village called Cuminestown. I was excited about this but then I was taken into a fairly dark room with my parents and asked to sit down. Dad told me that Auntie Nell and Uncle Bob had "*taken a fancy*" to me. They were wanting me to stay with them and be their child. He asked me how I would like that and seemed to think that I would be pleased. I asked if Gladys was going to the new house and when he said she was, I was upset and said that I wanted to go to the new house too. "*Gladys should not get to go if I'm not*", I told them. I think I must have made it clear that I did want to go to the

# From Barbados to Banffshire

new house and did not want to remain in the hotel with my aunt and uncle. My mother, having kept quiet throughout the conversation, stood up and said, "*Well that's that*". I like to think there was a sense of relief in her voice. I did not think much more about it and was delighted to start school in Cuminestown when still only four. Mum did tell me much later after I broached the subject with her as an adult that it was never her idea.

I can understand with my adult's mind that the new house was not very big, and I realise that my father would have been very concerned about the financial implications of having to bring up four children, when he did not have a job. He had been advised by his doctor that if he returned to live in the tropics, his life would be significantly shortened, as the hot climate was aggravating his health condition out there.

My aunt and uncle were quite well off and had been longing for a child. I have come to realise that in certain circumstances it was common practice for a child in a large family to be donated to childless relatives. Indeed, it was considered selfish not to do so. Although my Dad told me quite often that I had "*broken poor Auntie Nell's heart*", I never regretted being allowed to make the decision at the tender age of four, as to where and with whom I wanted to live. My mother was a warm, loving person who left us in no doubt that we were all equally loved. My aunt was more of a no-nonsense type of person, always busy, though caring in her own way. Dad's parenting style, like his sister's, was quite old fashioned. He was strict with us and very much the boss in our household.

Gladys, who was still a toddler, was also "farmed out". She went to the home of our dad's cousin, Agnes Campbell (Auntie Agnes), and her husband (Uncle George), for a few weeks while my mother was in hospital giving birth to Betty. We loved visiting them throughout our childhood, and later too. Auntie Agnes was a cheerful, welcoming person who baked lovely cakes and scones. I can still hear her kind voice and see her smiling face as we piled into her house for a visit. When we were told they were coming to visit us, we would sing "*The Campbells are coming Ho ro Ho ro*" as we rushed around tidying the house. We always had to tidy the house when visitors were coming.

## Crossroads Farm, Rothiemay

In 1949, Dad bought a farm one mile from Rothiemay, a small village fifteen miles from Banff. There was no electricity in the farmhouse, so we used paraffin lamps and coal fires. It was very cold in winter. Ice would form on the inside of our bedroom windows during the night. I do remember men coming to put up the electricity cables not long after we moved in. We had a pylon erected in one of our fields for which Dad was paid £8 per year.

## School Days

Margaret and I were enrolled into Rothiemay Primary school in the August soon after we arrived in 1949. Gladys and Betty were still under five so remained at home until they reached school age.

The classrooms at Rothiemay were bright and airy, and there was a welcoming atmosphere. However, some of the pupils taunted us saying that we were very rich and had "*bags of gold in the attic*". They, "*knew this to be true*", as we had come over from America! On relaying this piece of interesting information to my father when we went home, he soon relieved us of that misapprehension. We did bring bags of sugar, for the relatives, which were welcomed, considering sugar was still rationed for a while following the second world war. Some pupils would also say to us rather disapprovingly, "*Yer mither is posh*".

An added disadvantage was that we could not speak the local dialect. Although my father was quite fluent in "the Doric" when chatting with the other farmers, he always spoke the "Queen's English" to my mother. She had a hard time understanding the local farmers. My sisters and I, on the other hand, were taught the "lingo" by our friends, usually at dinner times in the school canteen. I soon learned the Doric with great enthusiasm. My accent is still not great, but I understand every word.

# From Barbados to Banffshire

My best friends in my class were Jean Reid and Nan Durno. I was grateful for their friendship. They remember me being a "*pathetic wee quine*" and thought I needed looking after. We are still good friends, and we meet for lunch at least once a year.

School days in 1950 Scotland could be quite stressful. Nobody had ever heard of "order marks" which was the only means of discipline administered at my mother's school in Trinidad.

The teachers used the belt quite freely and nobody was safe from the wrath of any of the teachers. Spelling was a particularly traumatic time, although I was a very good speller and usually had them all correct. Pupils who got 3 or more spelling mistakes out of 10 were given the belt. I felt sorry seeing the same boys or girls getting belted every morning. It was a very unpleasant experience. The teacher for primaries six and seven, Miss Farquharson, who was disrespectfully known as "Auld Fluff" seemed to enjoy wielding her offending weapon far too often. I got the "strap", as it was often called, for dropping stitches in my knitting on one occasion. The crime was not so much the knitting as the breaking of the rule "Thou shalt not speak in class", as I had asked the girl beside me for her advice on how to fix my knitting. I was so upset I vomited on her shoes. Other methods used for discipline were chalk throwing or being whacked with a ruler on the back of the hand. Gladys remembers getting the strap for having 3 spelling mistakes. The teacher told her she must tell our mother about her dreadful performance. When Gladys told Mum that she got 7 out of 10 for her spelling her reply was "That was very good - 70%".

The headmaster at the school, Mr Naughtie, had a baby son called Jim. He would run across the playground without a nappy on. I was one of several willing helpers who would respond to desperate cries from his mother, "*Will somebody please catch Jim?*" I was even allowed to put his nappy on if I was the first person to catch him. Jim attended Rothiemay Primary and Keith Grammar Schools as I did myself. He was in the same class as my youngest sister Avril. They are still in touch today.

# Chapter 7 – My Life Story

We were proud when we learned that Jim, a "Rothiemay loon", had become a distinguished international journalist and radio and TV personality. He is best known for having presented the "Today" programme on BBC Radio 4 for 21 years. While considering himself semi-retired he is still in demand having commentated on the Queen's funeral in 2022. Using his full name of James Naughtie, he is also a successful author and literary critic. He hosts a programme called "The Book Club" on BBC Radio 4, where new books are reviewed by a panel of readers. It is always very interesting.

## Life at Home on the Farm

Avril was born in May 1951 in Aberdeen Maternity Hospital. I remember the day she came home from the hospital. We gazed in wonder at this new life looking up at us from within a turquoise painted cot with nursery motifs which had seen better days. And yet, I was able to detect an atmosphere of slight disappointment as here was yet another girl. However, her rosy cheeks and sunny personality soon won our hearts. She became my father's constant companion as soon as she could walk.

Over the years Dad would remind me, especially when I asked for something like a bicycle, that if I had stayed with Auntie Nell, I could have had "ten new bikes". Dad appeared to have no idea that I would feel rejected by him being prepared to hand me over to his sister. Nevertheless, he was a caring Dad who took his responsibilities as a father very seriously. I think that the life I would have had, growing up in a hotel while being well catered for, would have been quite different to the life I experienced growing up on the farm. We had lots of chores to do like collecting eggs, and washing them, feeding the hens, mucking out the henhouses, picking potatoes, weeding carrots, and helping with the harvest. Without doubt, I would have had just as many chores of a different kind, like washing dishes, making beds, and setting tables, had I grown up in The Crown Hotel, Banff.

I completed my primary schooling at Rothiemay, and after sitting what was known as the "eleven plus" exam, I achieved the required pass mark to be allowed to attend Keith Grammar School in the

# From Barbados to Banffshire

"1 BC" class learning one language (French) as well as Commercial Studies. I had not quite achieved the pass mark which would have allowed me to study two languages in what was called the A class. I later learned that my father had been advised by the headmaster that as I was close to the pass mark for the A class, he could have appealed for me to join that class. Dad was of the opinion, at that time, that girls did secretarial work and got married so had no need for two languages. My youngest sister, Avril, who is eight years younger than I am, did pass the "eleven plus" for the A class at Keith and went on to study English Literature at Aberdeen University. I was oblivious and unconcerned as to what might have been and remained at school until I was sixteen, leaving with a modest clerk typist qualification. At least I can be sure I fulfilled my father's ambition for me. He never knew I later became a social worker after I had my children. We would have had some very interesting arguments.

## Hobbies and Leisure

I have always enjoyed singing from an early age. My first experience of singing in public was at a school Christmas party where I sang the hymn "See in Yonder Manger Low". I was seven years old and very nervous. I continued to be asked to sing at various local concerts and family parties. My parents paid for me to have singing lessons while still at school. I was awarded a certificate of merit from the Burns Federation for "Excellence in the singing of Scottish songs". I really enjoyed the pop music of the day and learned the words and music by ear while listening to the radio. I still remember the words of most of the pop songs of the time. My favourite singers were Alma Cogan, Dusty Springfield (I saw her live in Keith and have her autograph), Connie Francis and later, Joan Baez and Judy Collins. Elvis Presley was the love of my life when I became a teenager. I saw the Beatles in Keith before they were famous. I was not impressed, and my friends and I went to the cloakroom to fix our makeup while they completed their set. We thought they were scruffy looking. We had come to see Johnny Gentle. "Who?" I am a Beatles fan now and love their music.

# Chapter 7 – My Life Story

I enjoyed my teenage years in Rothiemay, cycling a lot, attending the local Youth Club, and going to dances in Grange, Keith and Huntly.

We got a new minister when I was just entering my teens. He was young, tall, dark, and handsome, and seemed genuinely interested in the youth of Rothiemay. He started a Youth Club, as well as a Bible Class which was well attended. I became the secretary for the Youth Club and enjoyed helping with the organising of parties and concerts. That new minister was Reverend Michael Dickie. He was born in Glasgow, went to school in Dundee and attended University in Edinburgh, so very much a city chap. He had a beautiful wife and young family, and it was quite a challenge for them living in a small village in Banffshire surrounded by the old-fashioned grandees of Rothiemay. My mother had a great deal of empathy for them, especially his wife, Marjory.

Of all the adults in my life, I consider Michael to have been the most inspirational person, for me then, as well as now. It is probably due to his influence, as well as my family background, that I am still a Christian. He encouraged me to train as a social worker and advised me to apply for the Children's Panel to gain appropriate experience. He was a great comfort to me, especially during the dark days of my son's illness and suicide.

Now 93 years old, Michael is still one of my dearest friends and Dave and I visit him as often as possible, considering he lives in Ayr which is a few hundred miles away. He is a widower and lives alone. I know he suffers badly from back pain and other physical disabilities, but he never complains and is a joy to visit. He still drives and finds this affords him freedom to get around. Michael is in the process of dictating his life story, with the intention of publishing it. He has had a long and very interesting life which I am looking forward to reading about. He has fond memories of his first parish of Rothiemay.

# From Barbados to Banffshire

When I was 16 years old, my friends and I went to the dances in Huntly Stewart's Hall. One of the local youths, Gordon Shand, had a "tattered tarpaulin covered" pickup truck which we would all pile into and then be driven to Huntly from Rothiemay for the dance. We sat on wooden benches and we got there safely somehow. On one occasion I was offered a lift home in a rather nice car by a chap I "fancied" known as Clarkie. He drove quite fast through the backroads of Huntly and managed to have a head on collision at an unmarked crossroads. I sustained a cut requiring stitches above my right eye and can remember as I regained consciousness thinking I had died but it was raining so I couldn't be in "heaven". I was taken to Huntly Hospital where my eyebrow needed several stitches. I still have the scar.

After the crash, the car was driveable and Clarkie was able to drive me home. I gave my parents a fright at the sight of my bandaged head. I spent a week hiding in my bedroom with a very swollen and bruised face, listening to LPs of "South Pacific" and "Carmen" kindly brought to me by our local minister, Michael Dickie. I thought I was going to look like that for the rest of my life so as I lay in bed, I contemplated a future making my home in a cave on the Knock Hill and only coming outside when it was dark. I would live the life of a hermit. The swellings did die down and as soon as I felt presentable, I announced my intention to join my friends going to the dances in Gordon's old truck. It was safer for me than Clarkie's expensive car, I told my parents. Dad looked at me in despair and said he had hoped I would have been taught a lesson by my experience and would not be gallivanting anymore. He told me that I caused him more worry than the rest of my sisters put together.

# Chapter 7 – My Life Story

## Early adulthood

After leaving school at the age of 16, I did clerical work for "Riddoch of Rothiemay", a local timber merchant, for about a year, while still living at home. It was owned by two brothers, Messrs William and Wyness Riddoch. Mr Wyness was in the office most days. His wife, Gerda, used to present the prizes at school. When I was still at primary school, I was slightly scared of her as I thought she looked like the wicked queen in "Snow White and the Seven Dwarfs". She was tall and slim, deeply tanned and wore bright red lipstick. Her eyes were heavily made up and seemed half closed when she smiled. She had long red nails, and wore her sleek black hair tied back into a bun. I was fascinated by her dangling gold earrings but at school prize giving day I would avoid eye contact while she handed me my prize. Mrs Wyness was always very elegantly dressed and she spoke with a Canadian accent. Very exotic for Rothiemay! She was a very nice lady really. She was also the Chief Commissioner for the Girl Guides of which I was a member. As I grew up I admired and respected her as I saw her quite often.

During my teenage years I remember being very afraid that there was going to be an atomic war; the cold war was a hot topic at that time. In order to prepare us for this eventuality, "One-in-Five talks" were offered to young people telling us what we could do to try to survive an atomic attack. These talks took place at the beautiful home of Gerda and Wyness Riddoch at Whitestones, Rothiemay. Mum also attended the talks held for adults in the local village hall. We were told that we would need to line the windows with tin foil to reflect the very bright light. We would also have to remove all inflammable items from the home and designate somewhere like the cupboard under the stairs as the safest place to be. I was concerned that we did not keep enough tinfoil in the house to cover all the windows. All these tasks were to be completed in four minutes as we were told to expect "A four-minute warning". A few years after we had been trained in how to survive atomic warfare, what was known as the "Bay of Pigs", or the "Cuban Crisis" happened in 1961-62. It was caused by a failed attempt by the Americans to overthrow the Communist government of Fidel Castro in Cuba. It was a very scary

# From Barbados to Banffshire

time indeed. John F. Kennedy was the President of the United States, and we were glued to the radio and TV listening to his speeches to find out if there was going to be a third world war. I was 18 years old. It took a long time before this fear of an atomic bomb coming to Aberdeen left me. Over the years I began to feel safer as the prospect became less likely. Rothiemay is approximately 40 miles from Aberdeen.

I find it deeply troubling to think that now, some sixty years later, we could be facing the same fears as we did then. My grandchildren are the same age as I was then. I am sad to think that their generation is having to experience the same anxiety about the world as I did.

## Work, Marriage and Children

After a short time doing the rather boring clerical work for the Timber Merchants' office in Rothiemay, I left to train as a GPO telephone operator, and got a job in Keith Telephone Exchange which was one of the last fully manual telephone exchanges in Scotland. It was more interesting and involved shift working and weekends. I got to know the local Keith people by their telephone numbers. Looking out of the Exchange window, we would say to each other things like, *"There's number 250 walking down the street, so that's why he isn't answering his phone." "I'm sorry, there's no reply."*

While still working in Rothiemay I was introduced to my first husband, Norman Murdoch, by his late sister Sheila, who worked beside me in Riddoch's office. He was the third son of a local farmer and was employed as a radio officer in the Merchant Navy which involved him travelling all over the world. I found this interesting and enjoyed getting letters from different ports such as Papua New Guinea, Belize and other distant destinations. When he left the Merchant Navy to take up a shore-based job as an electronics engineer in 1962, I moved to Edinburgh and stayed in digs with an Edinburgh widow, in Boswell Crescent. I did my own cooking and got terrible food poisoning from eating week old bacon. I did not have a fridge in my bedsit: don't ever offer me a bacon sandwich!

# Chapter 7 – My Life Story

I got a job working with Edinburgh Fire Brigade as a telephone operator, answering the emergency calls from members of the public reporting fires which required the attendance of the Fire Brigade. I was known as "Firewoman Weir" and wore a green "uniform"! That job was also interesting and involved shift working, including night shifts. It was quite exciting ringing the bell, for the firemen to slide down the pole, and clamber into the fire engines, usually looking half-asleep.

**Firewoman Weir**

Norman and I got married in Rothiemay Parish Church and the reception was held in the Gordon Arms Hotel in Huntly on the 4th of April 1964.

There were 100 guests and Gladys and Betty were my bridesmaids. Mum made their pink satin dresses. It was the custom at weddings for the groom to be given numerous glasses of whisky by the farmers attending the wedding. Norman was no exception and we thought nothing of getting into his father's car and him driving all the way to Elgin from Huntly for our honeymoon night in a hotel in Elgin. Drunk driving was not a criminal offence in 1964. He did not seem at

# From Barbados to Banffshire

all intoxicated to me but I don't think he would have passed a breathalyser had there been such a thing.

I had to leave my employment as a "firewoman" because the Fire Brigade did not employ married women at that time. Our first home was a room and shared kitchen in Hermitage Place, Leith, Edinburgh. I did have another clerical job for about seven months and then towards the end of 1964 we moved to Aberdeen to a first-floor tenement flat in Rosebank Terrace, as Norman's new employment as a radio technician at Aberdeen University required that he move to Aberdeen. I was pleased to be able to return to live nearer to my family and friends in Rothiemay, especially since I was already pregnant with our first child.

David was born on 21st January 1965 in Aberdeen Maternity Hospital. Winston Churchill was on his deathbed at that time, so the topic of the day was speculation as to when the great man would die.

Pamela was born in the Clenoch Maternity Hospital in Stranraer in December 1967 (it has since been demolished). She was baptised in Castlehill Parish Church, Ayr by Reverend Michael Dickie. We lived in the Stranraer area from 1966 until 1970 while Norman worked as a radio engineer at the former National Air traffic Services Radio Station at Galdenoch. We moved from Stranraer to Ayr in 1971 when the centre was closed. I enjoyed living in Ayr. Reverend Dickie, who had been the minister in Rothiemay when I was a teenager, was the minister at the Castlehill Church, which was nearest to where we lived. Not a complete coincidence of course. Judith was born in Irvine Central Hospital in Ayrshire in May 1972. It was snowing that week. Judith too was baptised in Castlehill Church by Reverend Michael Dickie.

Another house move took place, this time back to our home area of Aberdeen in 1973 due to Norman obtaining work as an Air Traffic engineer at Dyce Airport. It was good to be nearer to our families again, although Dad had already sadly died in 1971.

# Chapter 7 – My Life Story

I got a job singing with a dance band soon after we moved to Aberdeen. This was very tiring work and involved singing for five hours every Friday and four hours on the Saturday. It was with Ron Morrison's Dance Band at what was then the Gaiety Ballroom, on the Beach Front. There were no band rehearsals. I was handed the music sheets for whichever songs were in the top twenty and had to just sing them looking at the music sheets on the piano. I left when a new manager wanted me to do more interaction with the audience, such as sitting on men's knees. I am not that "precocious" Grandma! We moved to Westhill in 1976 and I continued to be involved in the folk music scene while studying for my social work qualification at Robert Gordon's Institute of Technology (RGIT).

In July 1982 I was awarded a qualification in Social Work (CQSW) at the then RGIT. I was employed in that profession by Aberdeenshire Council Social Work Department and worked out of Inverurie and Ellon offices. Although my work as a social worker could be stressful, I enjoyed the challenge and found it fulfilling. I worked mainly with children in Child Protection and then Adoption and Fostering. I still keep in touch with and meet some of my former social work colleagues regularly.

Norman and I separated in October 1981 mainly due to us developing different interests and "growing apart". I was an immature 17-year-old when we met and had rarely left the small parish of Rothiemay by the time we got married in 1964. We were living in Westhill at the time of the breakup, and I was attending RGIT in Aberdeen, studying for my social work qualification, so new horizons were beckoning. In 1981 I moved to Ellon with the children, who were by this time 16, 14, and 9 years of age, respectively. My mother lived nearby, which was the main reason for choosing Ellon to move to. Judith went to her house after school when I was at work, and we all enjoyed living closer to Mum. The divorce was granted in 1984 following the required two years of separation.

# From Barbados to Banffshire

## Life Begins at Forty, Well Almost.

I met my second husband David Wilkie in March 1982 on the day he arrived in Aberdeen to take up employment as a mechanical engineer in the oil business. He moved in to live with us in my flat in Ellon not long afterwards. He was born and brought up in Edinburgh. I enjoyed visiting his parents with him in Edinburgh. Sadly, they had both died by the year 2004. Dave's brother, Ian and sister Fiona are both younger than he is. I am fond of them both and get on well with them as well as their families. We meet as often as we can. Ian lives in Surrey and Fiona in Perthshire.

Dave and I were married in December 1986, and we live in a very old cottage in Aberdeenshire, 17 miles from Aberdeen. I am glad to say that despite some challenging times, Dave and I are still happy together. We celebrated our 35th wedding anniversary on 30th December 2021.

Dave and I share an interest in music and play mainly folk music as a duo. I had first become involved in folk singing while living in Stranraer and Ayr. I entered some competitions for unaccompanied solo traditional singing in Keith at a folk festival a few times without much success. I became disillusioned when a judge who was from a well-known traditional singing family told me I had a "drawing room voice", which he implied was not suited to traditional singing. However, when I entered a traditional singing (TMSA) competition in Aberdeen city in 1991, I was more successful. I was delighted to win a cup for singing two Burns songs. The judge was the well-known Scottish singer, Sheena Wellington. Meanwhile Dave and I had both become involved in the ceilidh scene. I am not a musician as such, I can play only basic guitar, so I played percussion and sang one or two songs acappella to give the band a rest in the course of a 4-hour ceilidh dance.

In 2003 I decided to become involved in an entirely different genre of singing. Barbershop, four-part close harmony singing with The Aberdeen Chorus of Sweet Adelines took over my life! I enjoyed every minute of it. I learned to sing harmony (baritone section) after initially singing in the lead section. The director of the chorus at the

# Chapter 7 – My Life Story

time was Gwen Hunter-Topp, a multi talented lady with an inspirational personality. Dave and I also became involved with a local Scottish country dance group (Aurora), not dancing, but playing in the band for the dancers. I sang and played percussion. It was quite a challenge singing in the strict dance tempo which was required for the dancers.

We were lucky enough to be able to travel abroad with the Aurora group to festivals in the Netherlands, France, and Italy. We had great fun and were usually accommodated in private homes where our hosts spoke very little English. We did this while I was still involved with the barbershop chorus. I travelled to competitions with them, meeting people from all over the UK, in Dublin, Plymouth, Birmingham, Newcastle, Nottingham, and Spain. We even won medals. I remained a member of the chorus for 15 years and was disappointed to have to retire for health reasons. I really missed the camaraderie.

During the lockdowns due to the Covid pandemic Dave and I were pleased to be able to continue with our music through Zoom sessions organised very competently by Bernie of Fyvie Folk Club. We have now resumed playing with fellow club members from Fyvie and Tarves Folk Clubs.

## David Alexander Edward Murdoch  21/01/1965 - 23/11/ 2008

David was my first-born, and only son. He was my parents' first grandchild, and his birth was welcomed with great excitement, especially by my sisters, my mother and both the Murdoch and the Weir families. David was baptised in Rothiemay Parish Church by Reverend George Harkess. From an early age he was a bright, talkative child who loved entertaining people with his ready wit. He had a lovely singing voice as a young boy and sang the hymn "All Things Bright and Beautiful" at my sister Betty's wedding when he was 9 years old. As an adult he

# From Barbados to Banffshire

had a powerful baritone voice. He enjoyed singing and playing the guitar.

School did not prove much of a challenge for David. He gained enough academic qualifications to be accepted for a physical sciences course at Robert Gordon's, Aberdeen without doing much studying.

During his late teens, he began to display symptoms of hypomanic behaviour and his life became a roller coaster of highs and lows. Just before his 21st birthday, he had to be compulsorily detained under the Mental Health Act in Cornhill Psychiatric Hospital, Aberdeen where he was diagnosed with manic depression (bipolar disorder). This was a huge blow for us all. He did manage to gain a Diploma in Physical Sciences at RGIT (see photo) but the illness dominated his life, and mine, intermittently, during most of his adulthood. Nevertheless, after developing an interest in all types of religion, he went on to study that subject and was awarded a Bachelor of Theology degree at Aberdeen University in 2005. We were all devastated when he took his own life on 23rd November 2008. It changed my life forever.

Although David never fully committed to any particular religion, he dabbled in them all including Mormon, Catholicism, Muslim, Presbyterian, Bahai and Episcopalian. His funeral was conducted by his good friend Father Emslie in St Margaret's Anglican Church, Aberdeen as a full requiem mass. It was very well attended.

After his death, I found numerous poems in his flat, some scribbled on pieces of paper and others typewritten. He had already given me some to type when he was alive. I compiled a poetry book called "Flying My Own Plane" with about 70 poems on a variety of topics. This was quite cathartic, and it helped me to better understand his very complex mind as well as come to terms with my loss. I sent the book to the mental health publisher Jason Peglar of Chipmunka Publishing. He was very encouraging and the book was published in 2009. It was first published as an eBook and later as a paperback. I experienced an enormous sense of pride when the first hard copy of the book dropped through the letter box.

# Chapter 7 – My Life Story

I was able to publish another book about David's thoughts on politics and life in general which he called "The Final Solution to the Problem of Evil". He had insisted it was not finished and he had managed to lose his laptop which contained a lot of his work, during a bipolar episode.

I have put up a Facebook page called "Flying My Own Plane", where details are available for anyone wishing to purchase the books. Proceeds have been sent to the mental health charities, SANE and more recently to the Scottish Association for Mental Health.

## My Daughters and Grandchildren

I feel blessed to have had my three children as well as my three adorable grandchildren. My two daughters Pamela and Judith had their children to their first husbands. They have both since remarried.

Pamela married Belgian professional violinist Dirk Van Loon in July 2012. Dirk played for BBC Wales Symphony Orchestra and taught violin in Aberdeenshire schools. Pamela is a qualified lawyer and since 2012 has set up and is presently running a small but successful property agency. Dirk has now retired and is able to help Pamela with her business, so they are kept busy. They live in a converted Icehouse near St. Cyrus beach along with their precious hens. It is about 40 miles south of Aberdeen.

Judith married Scottish seaman Christopher Rust in August 2020 He works on oil and gas installation safety vessels in the North Sea and is a qualified Bosun. Close family and friends were lucky to be able to attend their beautiful wedding in the large garden of their bungalow just outside Fyvie some 14 miles from where I live. This was in between strict lockdown periods so was extra special.

Judith gained a medical sciences degree (2/1 Honours in Nutrition) at Aberdeen University. She then studied for a post graduate diploma in Dietetics and qualified in 1998. Her first job was in Ayrshire (her birthplace), and she then advanced to become a Senior community-based dietitian and has been employed in that profession ever since.

# From Barbados to Banffshire

Pamela and Judith are both musical and sing well. Judith has been persuaded to sing at our local folk club on occasions but does not see herself as a folk singer. Pamela plays the violin and has played in Aberdeen symphony orchestras.

Pamela has two grown up children. Owen is studying Business and Spanish at Strathclyde University and is completing his degree in Spain this year. Owen takes part in Brazilian Ju-jitsu to keep fit. He has also learned piano and plays guitar as a hobby.

Roisin is presently studying for a degree in Medical Sciences at The University of Edinburgh. Roisin enjoys weightlifting and likes to keep fit. In her early teens she was a member of Aberdeen Academy of Performing Arts and has performed in public, dancing ballet as well as singing beautifully in a solo part.

Judith's daughter, Christina (16), a gorgeous redhead, is learning piano and is studying music as one of her main subjects at Turriff Academy. She has not yet made up her mind which career path to choose. Christina, Judith and Chris are devoted to their mixed breed Maine coon cat called Star.

I am immensely proud of both my daughters as well as their children. I am fond of both my sons in law and enjoy having them as part of the family. Dave and I are cat lovers. Our pet moggie is called Amber.

# Chapter 7 – My Life Story

## My Sisters

**Back Row; Christine, Margaret, Betty**
**Front Row; Gladys, Avril**

**Margaret** was born in Georgetown, Guyana in 1941. She was baptised in the Anglican church by our grandfather, Canon Turpin. Margaret started school in Banff, then attended Cuminestown and Rothiemay primary schools. After leaving Keith Grammar School, at the age of fifteen years, she left home and moved to Aberdeen for three years to train as a nursery nurse at Linksfield Pre-Nursing College. Her first job was in London as a children's nanny. She then moved across the sea to Northern Ireland to follow her chosen career in childcare. Margaret married Pat, an Irish artist, and painter/decorator, in Northern Ireland in 1967. She has lived there all her married life. Her last job before retiring was with a health trust as a care worker. She is an excellent cook, and her garden is beautiful, her pride and joy. She has also been a talented artist herself and has done some excellent portraits of family members. They do not have children.

175

# From Barbados to Banffshire

**I am the second oldest in the family.**

**Gladys** was also born in Guyana. She too was baptised by our grandfather Canon Turpin in the Anglican Church there. Gladys lives in Aberdeenshire with her husband Peter, a farmer, some 14 miles from where I live. They were married in 1970 and had six children, five sons and one daughter.

Their oldest son Peter married Heather In 2009. Their children are Elsa (12) and Alexander (9). They live in Reading. Peter has a BA in Quantity Surveying from R.G.I.T. in Aberdeen and a Post Graduate Diploma in Software Engineering from Napier University in Edinburgh. He enjoys cycling, golfing and hunting.

Craig is a Microbiology graduate. (MBChB, BSc hons and FRCpath) He has been employed most of his working life with the NHS as a consultant and lives near Kinross with his partner David. Craig is an avid gardener and enjoys playing classical music on the piano. His playing has been much enjoyed by our family when attending the family parties at Upper Crichie.

Milton has degrees in Rural Business Management and Economics both from University of Aberdeen. He runs a hunting tourism business in the Northeast of Scotland. Milton is a qualified Ju Jitsu instructor, speaks Italian and French and enjoys cycling and running.

Leanne is an Equine Science graduate and an animal lover She adores her dog Vero, her cat Nalla and her horses. Leanne is very artistic and spends her time when not riding her horses, working in her own painter/decorator business. She lives on a farm in Aberdeenshire, which she has renovated to a very high standard.

Paul died tragically at the age of 27 soon after graduating in Law, qualifying as a solicitor, and obtaining work in that profession. Paul was a lovely young man and is very sadly missed by us all. He was intelligent and very likeable. Paul enjoyed working on the farm. He also loved travelling in Europe.

Graeme, the youngest of the family, is a Sales Director for a Technology Company working between Edinburgh and London. He married Jenna in 2018 and they have two small children Wilbur (4)

# Chapter 7 – My Life Story

and Penelope (3). They have recently moved from Birmingham to Edinburgh.

Gladys is particularly happy around her grandchildren. She achieved the same Nursery Nursing qualification as Margaret in Linksfield Pre-Nursing College, Aberdeen. Gladys was employed full time as a nursery nurse in Clerkhill Primary School in Peterhead. After retiring, she opted to do supply work when needed in various schools in Aberdeenshire. Gladys is an excellent cook and loves to entertain her friends and family for dinner. A talented artist, she has painted lovely portraits of two of her children when they were quite young. She has hosted some enjoyable family parties, especially when Mum was alive and the children were younger. She enjoys choosing décor for the large farmhouse they live in, and her sense of colour and style is very much admired.

**Elizabeth** known as **Betty** married Jim, an insurance surveyor from Aberdeen in 1974. Their son John was born in Glasgow in 1979. They lived most of their married life in England.

A very talented knitter and crochet artist, Betty designed and knitted her own wedding dress. She also crocheted christening shawls for her nieces and nephews. Her lovely down to earth intelligent personality meant that all her sisters were proud to claim her as their favourite sister without the others feeling offended. She worked for the British Library in Yorkshire before she retired.

Betty developed diabetes when she was 11 years old. She coped very well with this condition. I had huge admiration for her stoic acceptance of it especially when she was not allowed to have ice cream and had to administer the insulin injections herself. She was diagnosed with Marfan's Syndrome much later. Betty sadly died in July 2018 one month before her 71st birthday. We all miss her terribly, particularly our long chats on the telephone as we did not see her very often.

# From Barbados to Banffshire

**Avril** was born in Aberdeen in 1951, and lives in Inverness with her husband William (Bill). They are both graduates from Aberdeen University. Avril achieved an MA Hons in English Literature. She taught English in Aberdeen and was Head of the Faculty of English and languages at Alness Academy before she retired. Avril is extremely well read and from a very young age always "had her nose in a book". She seemed to be able to switch off and concentrate on studying her subject of choice "English Literature" in a room full of family members, TV or radio blaring.

William achieved a double honours in History and Politics. He lectured in Public Administration at Inverness College UHI, before he retired.

Avril and Bill enjoy holidaying on the continent as often as they can. Avril is also an excellent cook and keen gardener. She is devoted to Alfie, her pet cat, as well as to Bill of course. They do not have children.

**Sisters at a Family Wedding 2009**

# Chapter 8 - The Genealogy Journey

## Maternal Genealogy Turpin Grant/ Gray/Rowley

My interest in genealogy developed very gradually. I was inspired mainly by my mother's West Indian family history and the fact that I was born in Guyana. Friends had often remarked that there was an interesting story to tell, but I did not realise until only a few years ago that the task of telling the story would fall to me.

After Mum died in 2008, I began to think more seriously about seeking out our family history; but it was not until our holiday in St Vincent and the Grenadines in 2014, that I made serious attempts to find out who she really was. In July 2014, following that holiday and heritage quest to those beautiful islands, I was contacted by my cousin Timothy Ince and his wife Eileen, saying they would like to visit us and hear about our trip. I told them what we had seen and where we had visited. As it happened, Tim and Eileen had been doing some family research themselves in the London Archives, also trying to find out who Joseph Turpin was. They handed me a sheet of paper which showed that an 18 month old boy called Joseph son of a black servant called Kate and owned by a Timothy Turpin had lived in Barbados in 1818. I was intrigued. Tim and Eileen had also found that the baptism records of our great grandfather, Edmund Adolphus, and all his siblings were listed in the London Archives, but there was nothing to connect them to this young Joseph described as "coloured".

All my mother's generation of close relatives had passed away, so I had no way of confirming or denying that this might be significant for our family. After mulling over what Tim and Eileen had told me, I couldn't resist the temptation to claim this Joseph as our ancestor. I started tossing it into family conversations now and again, to be met with replies of "No, not at all", or, "How interesting"! I got very excited about it.

In 2017, when we visited my cousin Lois in California, she told us that she had had a DNA test which revealed some African ancestry. I told her about our cousin Tim's revelation and she was as intrigued as I was. When I returned home from USA, I joined

# From Barbados to Banffshire

Ancestry.com and had a DNA test done. This gave me an analysis which included 2% African ethnicity.

I embarked on my genealogy journey with some degree of trepidation, fearing what disturbing revelations might await me but...... I thought I had already found my great great grandfather!

I later received the following extract from the Barbados Slave Registry which confirmed what Tim and Eileen had told me:

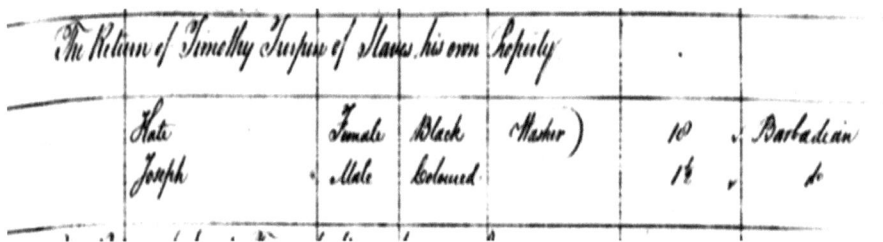

**Timothy Turpin's Slave Return**

**Barking Up the Wrong Tree Perhaps?**

Please forgive the pun. This account of my first genealogy experience will show the many pitfalls which can be experienced by the complete amateur in the genealogy process (see Appendix 1 - Turpin Family Tree). I began my journey feeling that I really wanted to claim this Joseph, son of Kate and owned by Timothy Turpin, as my ancestor. I allowed my imagination to take over with a romantic notion that my ancestor, Joseph Turpin, had been the offspring of a nice young man, alone in a strange country, who was about to be married. I speculated that his slave owning "bride to be", had gifted this beautiful, young, and enslaved Black woman, called Kate to be his housekeeper. He had, of course, according to my imagination, fallen in love with Kate, and he couldn't resist making love with her and fathering my great, great grandfather Joseph.... Just like in an old-fashioned movie.

# Chapter 8 - The Genealogy Journey

I had seen a TV drama based on a novel called "The Long Song" by Andrea Levy, set in Jamaica, which at first depicted quite a similar scenario to that which I imagined could have happened to Kate. In the drama it was implied that some planter's wives did not want to give birth to their own children. This was also mentioned in the book "Sugar in the Blood" by historian Andrea Stuart. I had been advised to read this book by Professor Sir Woodville Marshall (See Chapter 1 and Bibliography).

Timothy Turpin had not been a planter, but I later learned, he was likely to have been a merchant as he lived in Fontabelle, Bridgetown, which was the main centre of business in Barbados and is now the capital of the island. He did not appear to have any other slaves. Records show that Timothy Turpin married Sarah Hinkson on 31st December 1816; but there appears to be no record of there being any children of the marriage. Timothy's parents, Timothy senior and his wife Joanna were also registered in the Barbados baptismal records so, it appears, they had been in Barbados for several generations. The certain fact that, as an enslaved person, Kate had been deprived of her rights as a human being did concern me greatly. I found this disturbing and believed I owed it to her, to honour her memory. This was when my first thoughts to author a book which showed pride in my Black ancestry came to me.

When I thought more seriously of the true implications of the information that our great great grandfather may have been enslaved, I was appalled. I had read the descriptions of how African people, men, women and children were herded like animals in to slave ships to endure nightmare journeys with very little food, and horribly cramped conditions. I had also seen this described in several television documentaries.

When I joined the Facebook page for Barbados Genealogy research, I was pleased to have the help of professional genealogist Sandra Taitt-Eaddy. However, when I shared my belief with her that Joseph (son of Kate) was my ancestor, she tried to warn me that there was no real evidence of this. She did say that Sarah Hinkson,

# From Barbados to Banffshire

who married Timothy was from a planter family, which owned many slaves and that neither Timothy nor his parents were slaveowners to any extent. The Turpin name did not figure in registers of large slave owners or plantation owners.

However, a further slave registry entry was sent to me from Sandra. It showed that Timothy had bought some more slaves in his own name, and a young girl called Marianne had been born. Both Joseph and Marianne were on Timothy's slave register but were not registered as Turpin, which did concern me. In my ignorance I thought, if my assumption that he had fathered them was correct, they would not be registered as slaves. I was wrong of course. I later learned that it was common practice for the white plantation owners or managers in the West Indies to father children with Black, enslaved servants. In some cases, they would sell their own offspring to other planters. This could have been done in order to keep the peace with their wives. There was nothing to suggest that Timothy had done this. It was also disturbing to read that it was common practice for the white plantation owners, overseers or attorneys to consider themselves entitled to have sex with or even rape any women or girls, whom they either owned, or whose paths they had crossed for whatever reason. There was no requirement for them to give their offspring their name. Barbados law stated that children took their status from their mother.

I was disappointed when Sandra sent me an entry stating that Kate had died in 1823 when she would have only been about 25. Then the following year, Timothy also died while only in his thirties. I thought this would mean that Joseph and Marianna were left with Timothy's wife Sarah. or might have been absorbed into the Hinkson family's slave register. There was no stated cause of death, for either Kate or Timothy. I felt sad for these children who would still have been very young. With Timothy having died, did they ever have the name Turpin? What had become of them? There were no further records to reveal what had happened to them. Did Sarah keep them, or did she sell them and let them get their names changed to the new owners? My preferred outcome would have been that she married again, and their names were changed to her new husband's name. Either way this would take them out of the picture for me and my family. I felt I had no alternative but to abandon this story.

Throughout this time Sandra had been sending me information about another man called Joseph Turpin who had been an enslaved carpenter. She believed that this man was more likely to be my ancestor but.... he was never a bishop, so I was reluctant to accept this (see Chapter 1).

The day after we arrived in Barbados for our holiday towards the end of 2019, I received an email from Sandra attaching a very comprehensive document which she had spent several hours compiling. The document was entitled "Distinguishing the Joseph Turpins". Sandra knew I was interested in the boy Joseph mentioned previously, who might have been my ancestor. She detailed the two Josephs (one the son of Kate and one the son of Rebecca) in two columns. This document made it clear that there had been no further information about the first Joseph, son of Kate, after it was known that Kate and Timothy had died. Had I not been too distracted to study it properly, having just arrived in Barbados, I would have realised that Joseph, son of Rebecca, was more likely to be my ancestor. I know that Sandra became frustrated at how I was "wedded to the idea" that our ancestor, Joseph Turpin had been a bishop. She was right of course. Had this not been the case I would have realised that we had found the missing piece in the jigsaw, and the family myth could have been discounted before we left Barbados to return home in December 2019. In hindsight, an open mind would have been a great asset.

The marriage certificate which had appeared in Ancestry.com showed that, while Mary Jane signed her name M. J. Hinds, Joseph used the cross sign for a signature, indicating that he was illiterate (see Chapter 1). If Joseph, son of Kate, was my ancestor, I needed to find something to match him with the one in the marriage record. This did not happen.

# From Barbados to Banffshire

It is obvious that I made mistakes an experienced genealogist would have been able to avoid. I jumped to too many conclusions, went down blind alleys and did not make the best use of my holiday in Barbados or the help that was being offered by Sandra Taitt-Eaddy and Professor Woodville Marshall.

## Visits to the Black Rock Archives

One of our first stops on our holiday in Barbados was to the Black Rock Archives to see what we could find out. We asked about early Turpin settlers and had to complete forms to gain access to the relevant books mentioning the Turpin name. Cameras and mobile phones were confiscated, or it would have been easier to record more information.

The archivist showed us a population register which mentioned a Henry Turpin born in 1690 and a William Turpin born in 1688, both living in St Thomas Parish. We leafed through the heavy tomes laboriously, one by one, as they were brought to us by the helpful archive workers. We learned that Henry Turpin and William Turpin, possibly brothers, were amongst the first British settlers in Barbados in the 1600s. Henry Turpin is also mentioned in vestry meetings for St Michaels Church, as the "Overseer for the Poor", from 1659 into the 1660s. He was paid 774lbs of sugar for doing this task by the Church Warden, who himself received 3000lbs of sugar for his work. It's not clear whether this was a "lump" sum or a yearly salary. Henry was a member of the "Freeholders for the Parish".

Towards the end of our holiday, on the day before we were due to fly home to Scotland, we made a final visit to the Black Rock Archives. We reluctantly tore ourselves away from the beach, exchanging it for the sunless Archives where the air conditioning made us feel we were already back in Scotland.

We asked if there was a will for Joseph Turpin and there was one. He had died in 1881. Unfortunately, we were not allowed to view the will due to its poor condition. Had this been possible we would have known beyond all doubt that the Joseph, that Professor Woodville

# Chapter 8 - The Genealogy Journey

Marshall had been writing about, was my ancestor Joseph Turpin. This was because my great grandfather Edmund Adolphus was named as a beneficiary in this will.

We asked again about Henry Turpin and we were guided to look through the large volumes of wills. Henry died in 1704 and we had access to his handwritten will. In his will, there was a bequest to his grandson Henry Turpin, of ten acres of land plus "a negro slave to serve him all his days". His two granddaughters, Frances and Sarah, were left a slave girl each to "serve them till they died". Another grandson Tobias was left £50. I felt quite disgusted reading this casual reference to human beings as if they were mere chattels.

We also saw a will for a William Turpin which was similar. The son of his son, Timothy Turpin was to have £5. Also mentioned were his wife Sarah, a son William, and a grandson Timothy. We did not manage to get so many details of William as the Archives were just closing for the weekend by the time we found his will. It was a slow business getting information, and we were due to fly home the next day.

I was concluding from this information that our direct ancestor might have been that William Turpin, because of the familiarity of the names in the will. I was also assuming that this William was the son of the William Turpin mentioned in the will of William Turpin who was the early English settler of the 1650s and died in the early 1700s. Very confusing, but that is genealogy research, I'm afraid! The same names are repeated throughout the generations.

While studying these archive files it became clear that the names William and Timothy figured frequently in the Turpin family history. I think that although Timothy Turpin was likely to have been a relative, I now know that Joseph, son of William Turpin and Rebecca the enslaved servant, was our direct ancestor.

My experience has hopefully helped me to learn the lesson of how not to do genealogy research. I admit to spending the first six months of my journey jumping to conclusions and romanticising

# From Barbados to Banffshire

about people's lives in an effort to sanitise the horror that was slavery.

Joseph's wife Mary Jane Hinds has also caused some head scratching. Mary Jane was a common name in Barbados. We thought we had found her grave in Westbury Cemetery in Bridgetown as an ancestry record showed there was a Mary Jane Turpin buried there in 1904. We even visited there to look for it but only found the name and date in a book. Our Mary Jane lived in St Thomas not St Michael, so that Mary Jane Turpin was discounted when the record of the Mary Jane Turpin of St. Thomas burial was sent to me by Sandra.

I came across an entry, in "Family Search" the online genealogy research service, for a Mary Jane Hinds being born on January 23rd, 1796, to Abel and Elizabeth Thornhill Hinds in Barbados. If our Mary Jane was born in 1816, this other Mary Jane would have been about 20 years old; so, could have been her mother. No further confirmation has been forthcoming. Another red herring perhaps?

From further research through my membership of Family Search and discussion with my cousin Timothy and his wife Eileen, we have discussed the possibility that a man called William S. Turpin, who according to Family Search, was born in Deptford Kent, England on 29 July 1759 and died on 13 July 1820 in Barbados could be our ancestor. William is registered as having been a ship's cook on vessels sailing regularly between Southampton and Barbados and it seems plausible that he could have decided to remain in Barbados on one of his voyages. Perhaps the flamboyant plantation owner, Thomas Best, was a passenger on his ship during a voyage between England and Barbados. He may have tempted the ships cook with the promise of a more lucrative occupation as his plantation manager or attorney at New Castle plantation, Barbados.

# Chapter 8 - The Genealogy Journey

In Family Search, the Deptford, Kent English born William's parents were a William Turpin (1730-1822) and Elizabeth Hardacre (1730-1761). In Ancestry the same William is entered twice with the same birth date but different parents.

One Ancestry entry does give his parents as William and Elizabeth but there is also a brother called Benjamin with a birthdate of 22nd January 1760. It is inconceivable that Elizabeth could have had a live birth only six months after William was born, especially in those days.

The other Ancestry record names Deptford William's parents as Thomas Turpin and Ann Goldfrap. This record details that Thomas and Ann were married on 22nd April 1759 only 3 months before William was born, a "shotgun" marriage perhaps?

I think I need to discard English born William and Elizabeth as my ancestors and try to find out more about Thomas and Ann. I will have to leave that task to any of my descendants who are interested enough, or this book will never get to print.

There can be mistakes in both Family Search and Ancestry records. Anyone who is a member of these online organisations can make an entry and some of these entries can be conflicting or incorrect.

Sandra has always said that my ancestor, William Turpin, was born in Barbados but I have not found written confirmation of this. This could still be the case however, as the earliest Turpins did come from England. Further research is needed but for me this is my genealogical "brick wall".

So... just to confuse me, the amateur genealogist, there were possibly two Joseph Turpins of similar age, two Mary Jane Turpins of similar age and perhaps, more than two William Turpins of similar age!

# From Barbados to Banffshire

**My Paternal Genealogy - Weir//Turner/Forsyth/Webster Family.**

There were some sad stories in my father's family. Grandma Helen Weir lost her father when only six years old as well as three of her children who died early.

My father had been convinced that his sister Mary, who he was adamant he remembered dying of a cut finger at the age of two, was the child he observed his parents grieving over in her cot when she died. He said he was four years old at the time it happened. He repeated the story to us many times. However, I received a death certificate from Ancestry.co.uk as well as information from Family Search which states that Mary Jane Forsyth Weir died at the age of five months of meningitis in 1903. Dad would only have been two years old then. James Willcox, my cousin who is also a keen genealogist, has searched the child death records for Scotland and could find no other child called Mary Weir who died during the relevant period. He found only the five-month-old child I had the death certificate for. This is an example of how an early memory of a young child can be confused. Dad's true memory would have been of his parents weeping over his baby sister's cot. This must have been quite traumatic for him.

**Some Advice for would be Genealogists.**

Engage with your elderly relatives before their memory starts to fade. Ask them to write things down or ask their permission to record them reminiscing. I did try to do this with our adorable Auntie Bess Webster/Campbell, Dad's first cousin who lived to be ninety-five. On one of my visits, I decided to secretly record one of our chats where I made concerted efforts to steer the conversation to our deceased relatives. Not a good idea, Auntie Bess was much more inclined to tell us about what her neighbours had been doing and what had been happening in her hometown of Fraserburgh. If I had been more upfront with her and told her what I wanted, I'm sure she would have been much more forthcoming. She was a highly intelligent, forthright lady. You live and learn all too late.

# Chapter 8 - The Genealogy Journey

Family history is about much more than who was born where and when they died. I like to think that by writing this book I have brought them back to life in some way so that their descendants can know about them. It is amazing how so many had an interesting story to tell.

I have enjoyed my genealogy journey, but it would have been a lot easier if I had done even some of the above. So... for my family members who are interested in which illnesses of note may be passed down, here is what I have learned: in no particular order:

Alcohol Addiction, Osteo Arthritis, Depression, Bipolar Disorder, Strokes, Heart Disease, Diabetes, Marfan Syndrome, Cirrhosis of the Liver, Breast Cancer, Cancer of the Uterus, Brain Cancer, Ulcerative Colitis, Parkinson's Disease and GERD. The list is not exhaustive but is just what comes readily to my mind.

I am afraid that longevity did not run in any of our families to any great extent. The family members whom I found to have lived the longest are as follows: They are the exception, not the rule.

For the Turpins - Grace Turpin (Mum's oldest sister) lived to be 91.
For the Weirs - Peg Willcox (Dad's oldest sister) lived to be 95.
For the Websters - Bess Webster (Dad's cousin) also lived to be 95.

My advice to any budding genealogists out there would be: just get on with it. Prepare to be completely absorbed and even lose sleep. I am very glad to have done it. Most of all I am grateful to my ancestors for being such interesting people to write about.

Good Luck.

# From Barbados to Banffshire

## Appendix 1

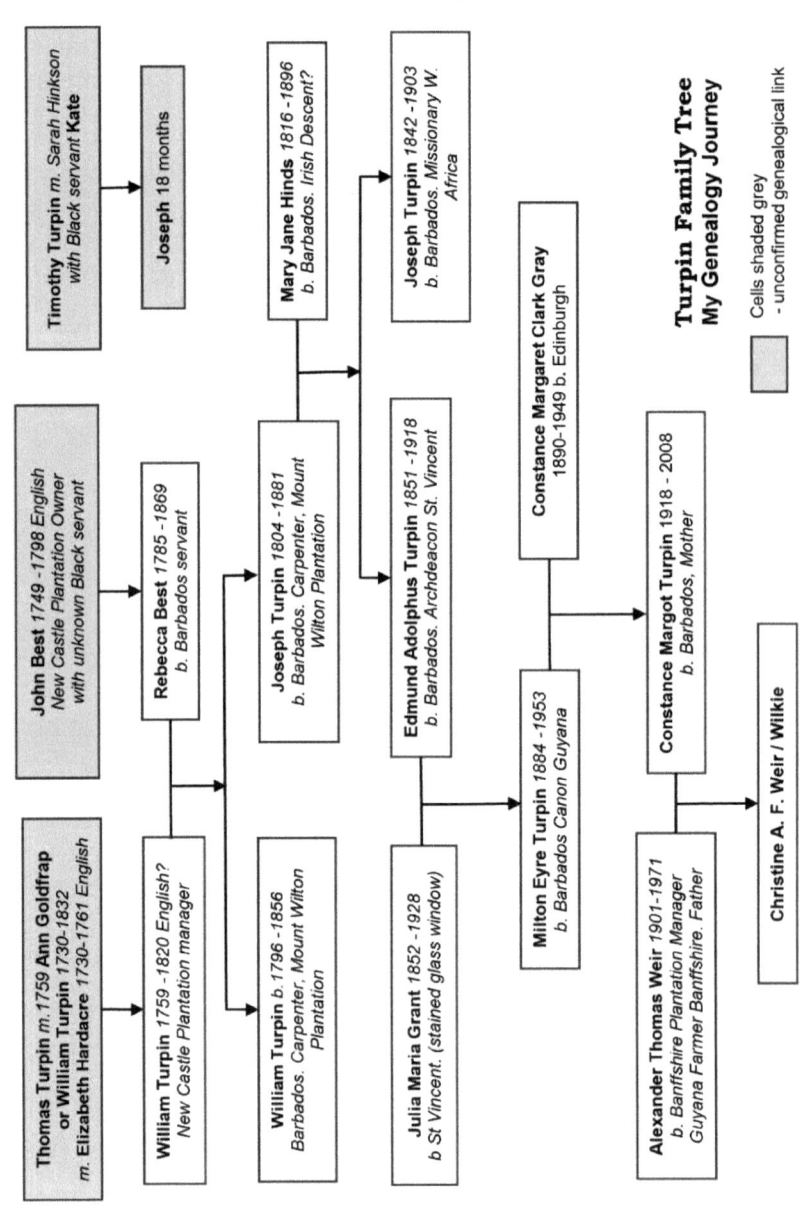

Turpin Family Tree
My Genealogy Journey

Cells shaded grey - unconfirmed genealogical link

Timothy Turpin m. Sarah Hinkson with Black servant **Kate**

Joseph 18 months

**Mary Jane Hinds** *1816 -1896 b. Barbados. Irish Descent?*

**Joseph Turpin** *1842 -1903 b. Barbados. Missionary W. Africa*

**Constance Margaret Clark Gray** *1890-1949 b. Edinburgh*

**John Best** *1749 -1798 English New Castle Plantation Owner with unknown Black servant*

**Rebecca Best** *1785 -1869 b. Barbados servant*

**Joseph Turpin** *1804 -1881 b. Barbados. Carpenter, Mount Wilton Plantation*

**Edmund Adolphus Turpin** *1851 -1918 b. Barbados. Archdeacon St. Vincent*

**Constance Margot Turpin** *1918 - 2008 b. Barbados, Mother*

**Thomas Turpin** *m.1759* **Ann Goldfrap** or **William Turpin** *1730-1832* m. **Elizabeth Hardacre** *1730-1761 English*

**William Turpin** *1759 -1820 English? New Castle Plantation manager*

**William Turpin** *b. 1796 -1856 Barbados. Carpenter, Mount Wilton Plantation*

**Julia Maria Grant** *1852 -1928 b St Vincent. (stained glass window)*

**Milton Eyre Turpin** *1884 -1953 b. Barbados Canon Guyana*

**Alexander Thomas Weir** *1901-1971 b. Banffshire Plantation Manager Guyana Farmer Banffshire. Father*

**Christine A. F. Weir / Wilkie**

190

# Appendices

## Appendix 2

### Places of Interest in Barbados Connected to the Turpin Family

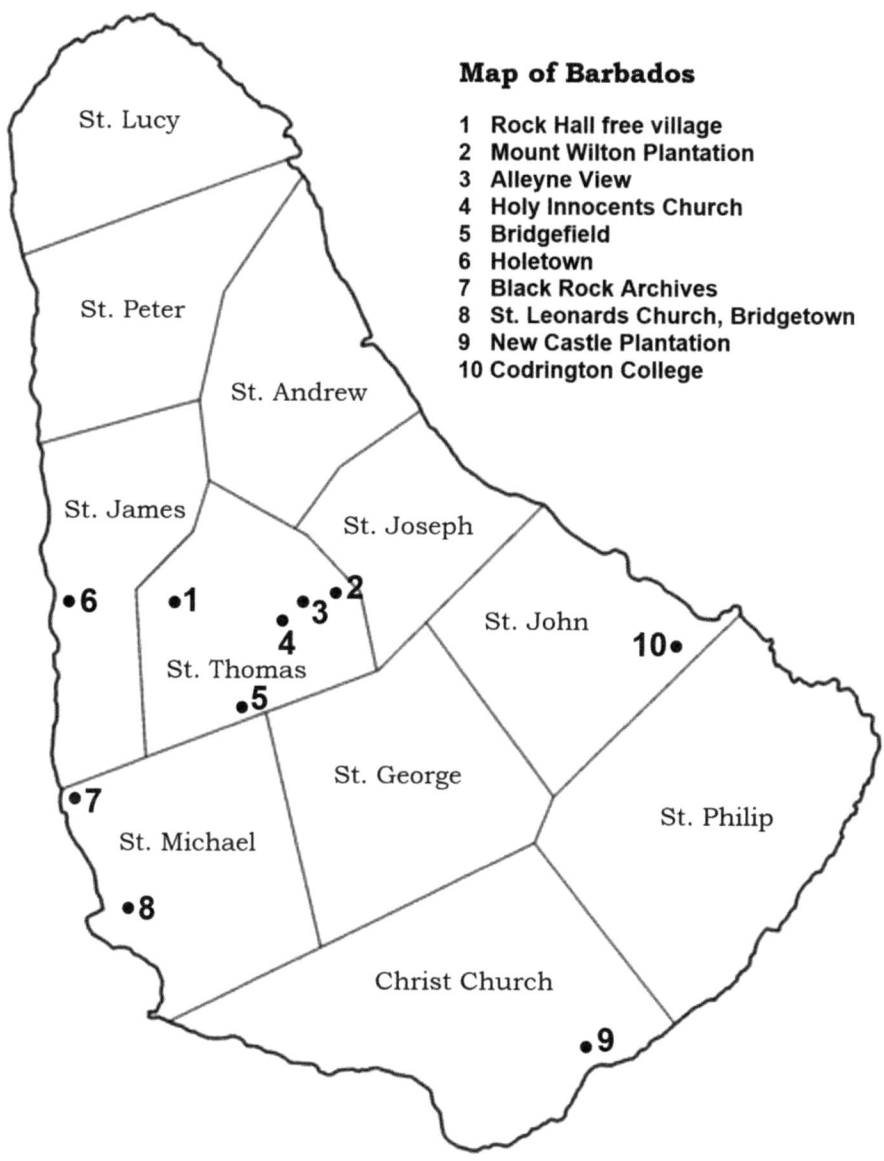

**Map of Barbados**

1  Rock Hall free village
2  Mount Wilton Plantation
3  Alleyne View
4  Holy Innocents Church
5  Bridgefield
6  Holetown
7  Black Rock Archives
8  St. Leonards Church, Bridgetown
9  New Castle Plantation
10 Codrington College

# From Barbados to Banffshire

**Appendix 3**

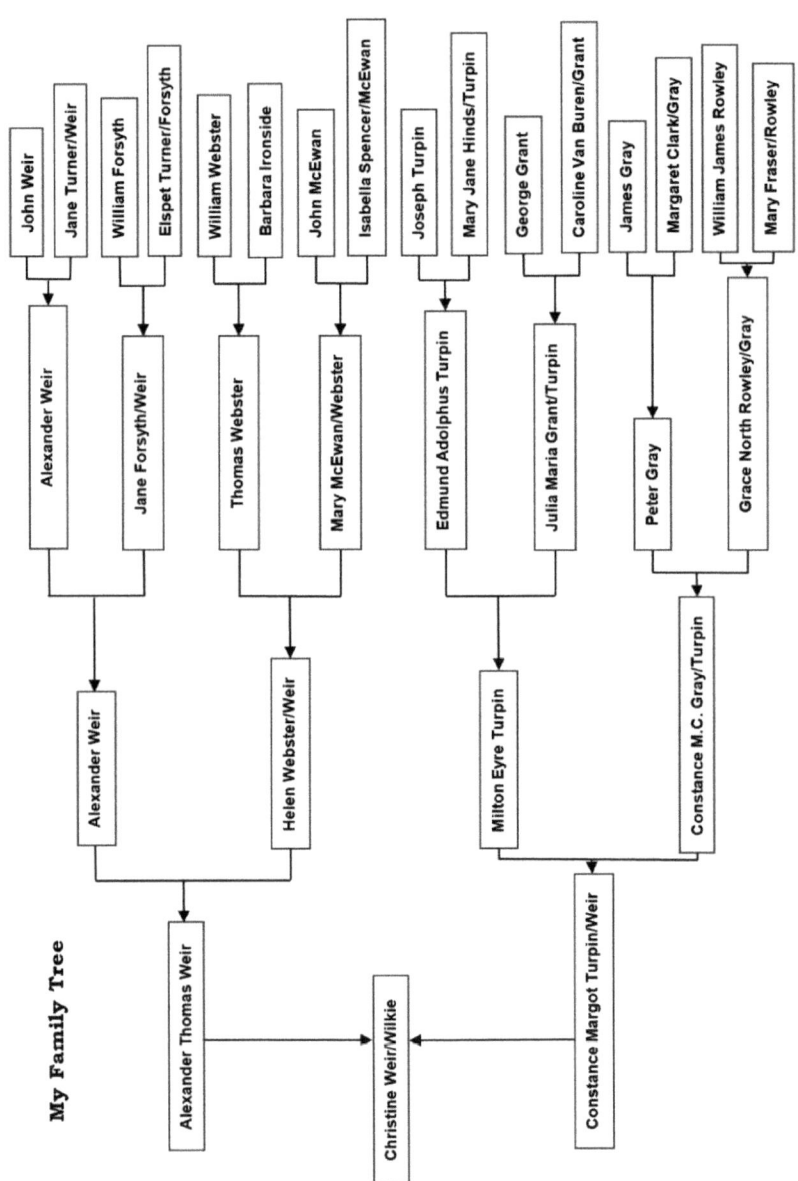

My Family Tree

# Appendices

## Appendix 4

## My DNA Analysis April 2022

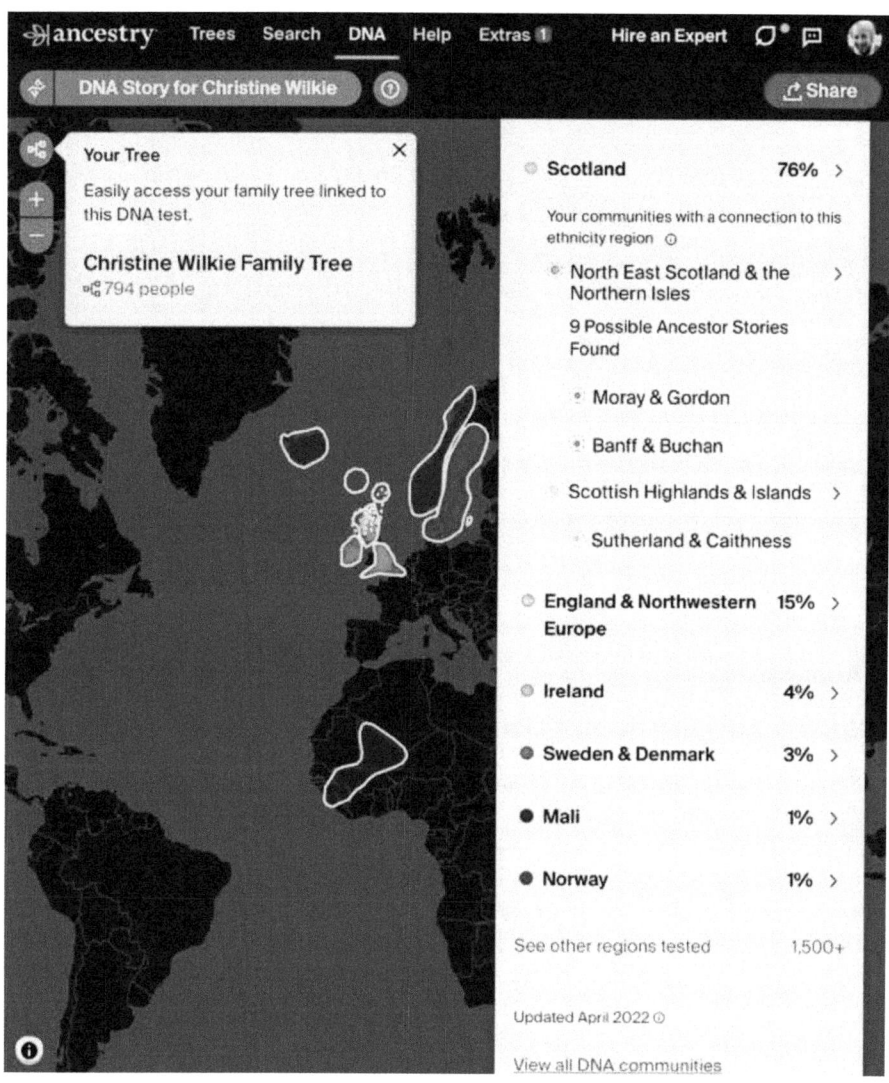

# From Barbados to Banffshire

## Appendix 5

## Article on First Freehold Villages in Barbados

**Bridgefield**, freehold village, is located on Highway 2, to the east of Edgehill and Cane Garden, to the south of Glendale and Dean's Village, and to the north and west of Bibby Lane.

This village, founded in 1841, was one of the first villages established by formerly enslaved persons, and it must therefore be classified as a Free Village. It also possesses some of the characteristics of a Bequest Village, because it was founded by nineteen of the men and women from the Mt. Wilton plantation who had each received the lump sum of £85 as a share of the bequest which Reynold Alleyne Ellcock had made them in his 1820 will.

Those nineteen individuals, led by William Turpin and Callop (Caleb) Dayrell, had pooled their resources to buy nearly twelve acres from Samuel LeGay Johnson. That land had been formerly a part of the Rugby or Social Hall plantation. The land was then subdivided into twelve lots, varying in size from half an acre to two and a half acres; and the lots were then sold at the previously agreed price to the nineteen members of the informal co-operative.

As a direct result, this sister village to Rock Hall was formed in January 1841. In 1918, the village contained twenty-eight lots which occupied fifteen acres; and the 1947 survey of peasant agriculture revealed the existence of twenty-five agriculture lots on nearly ten and a half acres.

The name can be found in the 1849 Police Magistrates' Half-Yearly Reports. That name presumably derives from an old bridge that spanned the gully which traverses the area. Significantly, William Turpin, one of the founders of the village, referred in his 1861 will to 'My place called Bridge Cottage--2 acres and 2 roods'.

## Appendix 6

## Church Attended by Mary Jane Hinds

Sharon Moravian Church is in the south of the centrally located Saint Thomas parish in Barbados. It was built in 1799 at the behest of missionaries.

The missionaries were from the Moravian Church, which originated in the Czech provinces of Bohemia and Moravia. In 1732, the church launched a global mission, going first to the Caribbean. Arriving in Barbados in 1765, the Moravians sought to bring Christianity and education to the slaves, and were the first Europeans to encourage slaves to join their congregations.

The Sharon church building is unspoilt by modernisation. Its architecture is strongly influenced by that of the parts of Europe from which the Moravian missionaries came.

*Source - Wikipedia and Sharon Moravian church website*

# Appendices

## Appendix 7

### Information on Thomas Best.

Slave-owner on Barbados, but dying in Worcester, England c. 1829. He had killed Lord Camelford in a duel in 1804, and went on to marry Lady Emily Stratford, daughter of the Earl of Aldborough, from whom he became estranged (1st Lord Camelford was Thomas Pitt, nephew of Lord Chatham and cousin of Pitt the Younger (1)).

Administration of the will of Thomas Best of Island of Barbados [entered in Barbados in 1829] was granted 25/03/1837 to John Stratford Best of Wilton Crescent, party to a Chancery suit (the grant showed Thomas Best as late of the City of Worcester). In the will, made in 1829 Thomas Best said he was about to journey to England. He gave a detailed account of the indebtedness of his brother John Parry Best, whose Fairey Valley estate he said he had recently purchased from Chancery and whose New Castle estate he [Thomas Best] was seeking to populate with enslaved people.

*Source.*
*University College London (UCL) The Centre for the Study of the Legacies of British Slavery*
*(1) Official Boconnoc House web site*

*Lately.* At the Blanquetts, near Worcester, aged 48, Thomas Best, esq. the antagonist with Lord Camelford in the duel behind Holland House, March 7, 1804, which proved fatal to his Lordship. Lord Camelford, it was stated in a pamphlet published in his defence, was principally urged to the meeting by "an idea that his antagonist was the best shot in England." A coroner's jury returned a verdict of "wilful murder against a person or persons unknown." The same year had not elapsed when, on Christmas day, Best married Lady Emily Stratford, daughter of the late and niece to the present Earl of Aldborough. She afterwards eloped from him, when in the King's Bench, with a Mr. Henry, to whom she was subsequently united. Mr. Best, whose fortune consisted chiefly of West India property, when very young became deeply involved, and was for some time an inhabitant of the King's Bench rules. He has left a son who is a Captain in the army.

*Source; Gentleman's Magazine Vol. 146 (1829) p. 285.*

# From Barbados to Banffshire

## Appendix 8

### Entry from Anglican Church Records
### For Milton Eyre Turpin

TURPIN, MILTON EYRE, REV.
(Photo No. 459)
Vicar of SS Simon and Jude, West Coast, Demerara.
Resides at St. Simon's Vicarage, West Coast, Demerara.
Born 14th August, 1884 in Barbados to Rev. Edmund
Adolphus Turpin, Archdeacon of St. George'
Cathedral, St. Vincent, B.W.I., and his wife Julia, né
Grant.
Educated at St. Vincent Grammar School, and Codringtor
College, Barbados, B.W.I.
Is an L.Th. (Durham) 1907.
1907 – Deacon.
- Assistant Curate of Christ Church, Georgetown.
1909 – Priest.
1910 – Assistant Curate of All Saints', New Amsterdam.
1910 - 1 – Acting Rector of All Saints' New Amsterdam.
1911 - 2 – Acting Chaplain, to H. M. Penal Settlement
Mazaruni.
1911 - 7- Priest-in-Charge, Bartica Mission, Essequibo
River.
1917 - 21 – Vicar of St. Saviour, St. Andrew's Parish
Barbados, B.W.I.
1921-35 – Rector of St. Michael's, Fort Wellington, Wes
Coast, Berbice.
1925-30-1 – Acting Priest-in- Charge of Bartica Mission
Essequibo River.
1931 – Acting Vicar of Belladrum.
1935 – Present appointment.
Was a Justice of the Peace for the County of Berbice and
Commissioner of Oaths to Affidavits.
Married 14th August, 1914, Constance Margaret Clark
Gray.
Has three sons and four daughters.

# Appendices

## Appendix 9

### The Right Honourable the Lord Gray of Contin

Born 28 June 1927 died 14 March 2006
Minister of State for Scotland 13/6/1983 – 11/9/1986
Minister of State for Energy 7/5/1979 – 13/6/1983
Member of the House of Lords - Lord Temporal – 4/7/1983 – 14/3/2006
Member of Parliament for Ross and Cromarty 18/6/1970 – 13/5/1983

James Hector Northey "Hamish" Gray, Baron Gray of Contin, PC, DL Scottish Conservative politician and life peer.

Gray was born in Inverness on 28 June 1927 and was educated at the Inverness Royal Academy. His father owned an Inverness roofing firm. He was commissioned into the Queen's Own Cameron Highlanders in 1945 and served in India, during partition. He married Judith Waite Brydon in 1953 and they had two sons and a daughter. He was elected as an Independent member of Inverness Council in 1965 and at the 1970 general election he was elected to Parliament as the Conservative and Unionist Party Member of Parliament (MP) for Ross and Cromarty. He was appointed to the Whips' Office in 1971, and he served as a front bench Energy spokesman (1975–1979). [1]

In 1976 he voted with the Labour government in favour of devolution, defying his party's three-line whip. Next day he offered his resignation to Margaret Thatcher, explaining that the Tories failure to support an elected Scottish assembly could lead to the party's demise north of the border. She refused to accept it. Upon the Conservatives' return to government in 1979, he was appointed as the Minister of State for Energy under David Howell. He was responsible for North Sea oil and gas developments, sympathetic to the continuation of Labour's nationalised British National Oil Corporation. Before the 1983 election, the Liberal-leaning Isle of Skye was added to Gray's seat and the aluminium smelter at Invergordon closed down.[2]

In the 1983 general election, he was defeated in the new Ross, Cromarty and Skye constituency by the SDP candidate Charles Kennedy. He was made a life peer in 1983, taking the title Baron Gray of Contin, in the District of Ross and Cromarty, and was Minister of State for Scotland from 1983 to 1986. He served Inverness as Deputy Lieutenant (1989), Vice Lord Lieutenant (1994) and Lord Lieutenant (1996–2002). He died on 14 March 2006 at a hospice in Inverness after a long battle with cancer. [1]

References:1. *From Wikipedia "Hamish Gray, Baron Gray of Contin"*
2. *Obituary by Andrew Roth in The Guardian 21 March 2006*

# From Barbados to Banffshire

## Appendix 10

(Direct ancestors are typed in **bold**)

### Maternal Ancestors; Turpin Family Details

My mother's paternal great great Grandparents are believed to be **William Turpin** 1759 - 1820 who bought enslaved **Rebecca Best Turpin** from **Thomas Best**.

**My great great Grandparents:**

**Joseph Turpin** 1804 - 12/5/1881 m. 4/4/1839 **Mary Jane Hinds** 1816 - 1896
Children:
1. Sarah Jane 13/8/1840 - 6/10/1908 m. Alfred Bonthrone Lind.
   Children: Margaret Olivia, Alfred Louis, Helen Isadore, St. Clair and Henry
2. Joseph William Thomas 24/9/1842 - 20/5/1903 m. Julia Rosamund Meyer.
   Children: Julia Chittendon, Winifred Josephine and Fred
3. Ann Euphrasia. b. 21/11/1844
4. Malvinia. b. 28/1/1847
5. Albert Augustus b. 28/9/1848
6. **Edmond Adolphus** 11/2/1851 - 1/12/1918
7. Frances Mary Jane b. 25/8/1853
8. Alfred George b. 21/6/1855
9. George Eyre Linsey b. 31/10/1857
10. Eva Margaret b. 12/6/1860

**My great Grandparents:**

**Edmund Adolphus Turpin** m. **Julia Maria Grant** 22/9/1852 - 1/4/1928
Children:
1. Guy Edmund 22/7/1872 - 6/10/1912
2. Ernest Albert 12/1/1879 - 18/3/1923
3. Cyril Anderson 6/6/1880 - 17/4/1957. m. Ruby Smee
4. Rosalie Agnes 31/1/1882 - 21/9/1919
5. **Milton Eyre** 14/8/1884 - 14/9/1953
6. Edith Gertrude 17/6/1886 - 31/1/1935. m. Cecil Edward Brisbane
   Children: Joy, Rosalie Dulcie, Antoinette and Joan
7. Stella Lister 30/9/1887 - 18/2/1954. Married Charles Parkinson Stout
   Children: Charles Lister, Cyril Edmund, Ivor Parkinson, Sheila Mavis and Keith
   Sheila Mavis married John Ince. Children: Timothy and Jeremy
8. Charles Vivian 27/1/1889 - 31/12/1975. Married Mavis Sealey
   Son: Ernest Charles Sealey Turpin
9. Sybil Alice 1/10/1890 - 1945. m. James Punnet
   Children: Ken, Valarie and Ernest

**My Maternal Grandparents:**

**Milton Eyre Turpin** m. **Constance Margaret Clark Gray** (27/2/1890 - 1949)
1. Grace Julia 1/101915 – 20/10/2008
2. Gertrude Daphne 17/061917 - 21/05/2004 m. Roy Asdaile Simpson
   Children: Clive, Lois Ann and Alec Nevile
3. **Constance Margot** 13/10/1918 - 10/7/2008

# Appendices

4. James Edmund Michael 23/11/1921 - 14/04/1971 - m. Phoebe Langford Rae
   Children: Raine, Toni Jane and Simon
5. Christine Maude Eyre 19/6/1925 - 15/2/2014. m. John Carpenter
   Children: Pamela, Byron, Margaret and Carole
6. Milton Everett 26/6/1926 - 26/8/2007 m. Edna Eley
   Children: Linda, Fay and Milton
7. Guy Oswald Garnet 26/9/1932 - 26/11/2016 m. Sally Guy
   Children: Jude, Lucinda, Milton, Connie, Mary and Grace
**My Parents; Constance Margot** m. **Alexander Thomas Weir** 25/4/1901 -
26/3/1971. Children as detailed see Weir Family Details.

**Maternal Ancestors; Grant Family Details**

**My great great great Grandparents:**
**Charles Grant (Major)** 1785 – 1828 m. **Mary Ann Hasler** b.1790
Children: **George Grant** 1813 – 1856, Charles Henry Grant 1814 - 1874, and
Louisa Ann Grant 1815-1892
**My great great Grandparents:**
**George Grant (Reverend)**1813 - 1856 m. **Caroline Van Buren** 1821-1899.
6 Children including **Julia Maria Grant** 1852 - 1926
**My great Grandparents:**
**Julia Maria Grant** m. **Edmund Adolphus Turpin**

**Maternal Ancestors; Van Buren Family Details**

**My great great great Grandparents:**
**John James Henry Van Buren** 1788 -1858 m. **Deborah Arindell Ruan**

**Maternal Ancestors; Gray Family Details**

**My great great great Grandparents:**
**Hugh Gray** 1813 – 1881 m. **Mary Matheson** 1811 – 1883
Son: **James Gray** 1841 -1908
**My great great Grandparents:**
**James Gray** m. **Margaret Clark** b.1835
Children:
1   Isabella b. 1853
2   Alexander b.1858
3   **Peter Gray** 1863-1900
4   Murdo Gray 1866 -1933
5.  James Gray 1869-1949 m. Anne
Children: Peter, John 1904 – 1905 and Northey Gray m Bunty. Son: Hamish Gray
**My great Grandparents:**
**Peter Gray** m. **Grace North Rowley** 1868 – 1907
Children: Mary Fraser (Mamie) Grace Christian, (Chris), **Constance Margaret
Clark** 1880 – 1949, James Thomas 1895 – 1917
**My Grandparents:**
**Constance Margaret Clark** m. **Milton Eyre Turpin**. See Turpin Family Details.

# From Barbados to Banffshire

**Maternal Ancestors; Rowley/ Fraser Family Details**

**My great great grandparents:**
**Mary Fraser** 1841 – 1875 m. **William James Rowley** 1845 – 1919. One daughter.
**My great Grandparents:**
**Grace North Rowley** m. **Peter Gray**
When **Mary Fraser** died **William James Rowley** m. Annie Watson. 13 children.

**Paternal Ancestors; Weir Family Details**

**My great great great grandparents:**
**James Weir** 1776 - 1825 m. **Jean Barber** b. 1778
Children:
1. Anne Weir 1804 -1888
2. **John Weir** 1804-1874
3. Margaret Weir 1806 - 1826.
4. Jean Weir 1808
5. Ann Weir 1810 - 1888
6. Elizabeth (Betty) Beatrice Weir 1812 - 1899
7. James Weir 1813
8. Isabel Weir 1816 – 1890
9. Duff Weir 1820
10. Janet Weir 1823.
**My great great grandparents:**
**John Weir and Jane Turner** 1811-1895. (daughter of **Alexander Turner** and **Margaret McConachie**)
Children:
1  Margaret Weir 1830-1901
2  **Alexander Weir** 1832-1908
3  Jane Weir 1834-1916
4  John Weir 1838
5  James Weir 1841-1916
6  Ann Weir 1846-1937
7  Mary Weir 1852-1859
**My great grandparents:**
**Alexander Weir** m. **Jane Forsyth**, (1842 - 1930) (daughter of **Elspet Turner** and **William Forsyth**)
Children:
1. William Wilson b.1863 (father Charles Wilson?)
2. Jeannie Turner Weir 1867 - 1923,
3. Jane Turner Weir 1868 - 1895
4. John Weir 1870 -1949
5. Margaret Weir 1872 - 1936,
6. **Alexander Weir** 1874 - 1941
7. James Weir b.1876
8. Robert Weir 1879-19319.
9  Charles Smith Weir 1883-1922

# Appendices

**My grandparents:**
**Alexander Weir** 1874-1841 m. **Helen Webster** 1877-1962 (daughter of **Thomas Webster** and **Mary McEwen**, for Webster family details see Chapter 6 Part 2)
Children:
1. **Alexander Thomas Weir** 25/4/1901 - 26/3/1971
2. Mary Jane Forsyth Weir Jan1903 - July1903,
3. William James Weir 1905 -1939
4. Margaret Bella (Peg) Weir 1906 - 2001, m. Hilton Leonard Willcox
   Children: Hylton, Ian, Margaret.
5. Helen McConachie (Nell) Weir 1908-1972, m. Robert Miller
   Adopted son Wallace
6. Frances Forbes. Weir 1910 - 1978
7. Alice (Bunty) Weir 1913-1945 m. Forbes Catto. Twins did not survive.
**My Parents; Alexander Thomas Weir** 25/4/1901 - 26/3/1971 m. Constance Margot Turpin 13/10/1918 - 10/07/2008
Children:
1. Margaret Helen Weir / b.1941
2. **Christine Alexe Frances Weir/Murdoch/Wilkie** b.1943
3. Gladys Margot Weir b.1946
4. Elizabeth Mary Morrison Weir 31/08/1947 - 18/07/2018
5. Avril Constance Miller Weir b.1951

# From Barbados to Banffshire

Bibliography

"Sugar in the Blood: A Family's Story of Slavery and Empire" by Andrea Stuart. Publisher, Portobello Books, 2012

"The Civilised Island, Barbados: A Social History, 1750-1816" by Karl S. Watson, Publisher K. Watson, 1979

"The Irish Slaves" by Rhetta Akamatsu, Publisher CreateSpace Independent Publishing Platform, 2010

"To Hell or Barbados, the Ethnic Cleansing of Ireland" by Sean O'Callaghan, Publisher Brandon, 2001

"Rock Hall, St. Thomas: A Free Village in Barbados" by Professor Sir Woodville Marshall, in Journal of Caribbean History 41:1&2, 2007

"Guyana – The Bradt Travel Guide" by Kirk Smock, Publisher Bradt Travel Guides, 2011

The Secret Diaries Of Miss Anne Lister: Vol. 1: I Know My Own Heart (Virago Modern Classics), by Anne Lister edited by Helena Whitbread, Publisher Little Brown Book Group, 2010

"Travels by Command" by Doctor Hilton Willcox unpublished. Typed by Lucia Willcox.

"Flying My Own Plane" by David A. E. Murdoch A book of poems published by Chipmunka Publishing, 2009.

"The Long Song:" by Andrea Levy - published by Headline review in 2011.

"Little Women" by Louisa M. Alcott.

# Acknowledgements

I would like to thank the following people who have shared their knowledge with me and helped and encouraged me to write this book:

Sandra Taitt-Eaddy, Caribbean genealogy expert for her initial interest and ongoing Barbados research from start to finish.

Sir Woodville Marshall, Professor Emeritus of History at the University of West Indies in Barbados. His study of the free villages in Barbados led me to the intriguing back story about my ancestor Joseph Turpin. It was an honour to meet him in person in 2019 and have his ongoing support through emails during the ensuing 3 years.

My friend since 1968 Ilene Menzies (B.Ed.) for her help to get me started and make sense of the story of the Josephs. She has given me the benefit of her previous experience with writers' groups. Her proof reading, advice re content. and editing. (in person and by telephone) has been invaluable.

My sister Avril Robertson (MA Hons (English Literature) for agreeing to be proof-reader in chief. Her inbox must be polluted with as many drafts as mine is. Also, for many hours spent on the phone. Avril lives in Inverness which is 100 miles away from where I live. We do not see each other nearly enough.

My cousin Jean Martin for her comprehensive research on the Webster family. She has also helped with some proofreading. Jean attended the University of Aberdeen where she gained an MA and subsequently became a teacher of English.

My sister Gladys Ferguson whose memory for family stories is superior to mine. She has also read some chapters and kept me right on a number of aspects of our shared family history.

My cousin Timothy Ince and his wife Eileen for being the first relatives to raise the possibility of our mixed ethnicity and set me on

# From Barbados to Banffshire

this journey. They have also helped to enhance the family history of the Turpins by providing old letters and photographs.

Patricia Turpin has also helpfully sent me family photographs and information for the Turpin Family Tree.

I am grateful also to the people who have read chapters and made helpful comments: namely

Ray Inkster, James Naughtie, Reverend Michael Dickie, Alison Green.

Cousins Lois, Margie, Fay and Lucinda, for contributing to their parents' profiles. They have helped me to bring their parents to life.

Aunt Phoebe for her help with Uncle Michael's profile.

My cousin James Willcox for helping me stick to the facts regarding the Weir family.

My newly found cousins who share my DNA according to Ancestry. Their willingness to share their research is appreciated.

Bruce Coull-USA (Turpins), Sandra Gamble-Australia (Grants), Caitlin Parr-NZ (Turpins), William Wallace-Australia.(Websters)

My sister-in-law Rhona Wilkie for initially formatting and putting the chapters together. She has used her past experience in graphic design and is responsible for the design of the book cover.

My husband Dave for putting up with my obsession to "get it done". His attention to detail towards the final days of completing the book has been stressful but necessary. Dave has done most of the final formatting as well as a lot of proof reading for the book. The diagrams for family trees and the map of Barbados are also his creations.